Golden Fleece

Golden Fleece

By HUGHIE CALL

ILLUSTRATED BY PAUL BROWN

UNIVERSITY OF NEBRASKA PRESS
LINCOLN AND LONDON

Introduction copyright © 1981 by the University of Nebraska Press
Manufactured in the United States of America

First Bison Book printing: 1981
Most recent printing indicated by the first digit below:
1   2   3   4   5   6   7   8   9   10

Library of Congress Cataloging in Publication Data

Call, Hughie Florence, 1890–
    Golden fleece.

    Reprint of the 1942 ed. published by Houghton Mifflin, Boston.
    Includes bibliographical references.
    1. Call, Hughie Florence, 1890–   . 2. Ranch life—Madison River Valley.
3. Sheep—Madison   River   Valley.   4. Madison   River   Valley—Biography.
5. Ranchers—Madison River Valley—Biography.   I.   Title.
F737.M24C34   1981   978.6′663   80–39781
ISBN 0–8032–1413–8
ISBN 0–8032–6308–2 (pbk.)

Reprinted from the original edition, Riverside Press, 1942.

For WEZIE
who loved this valley

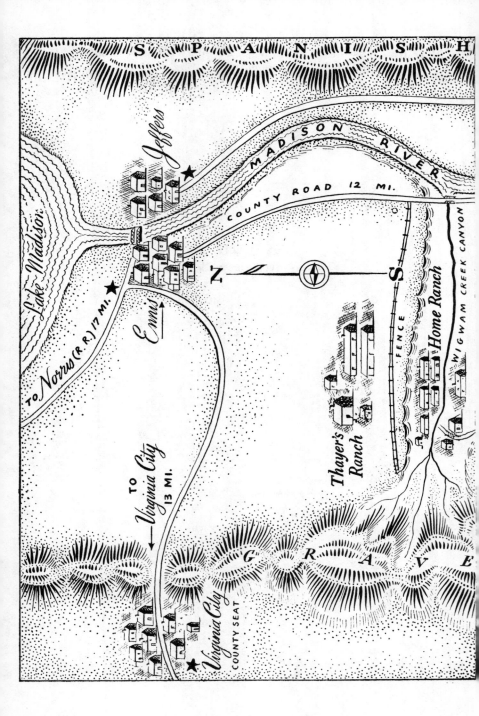

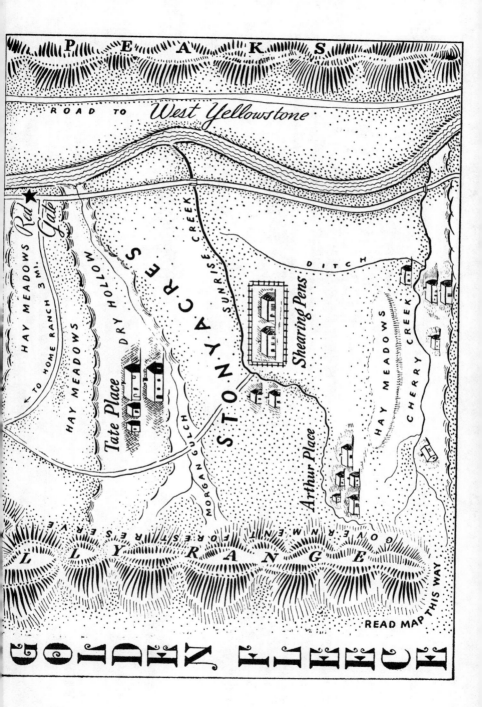

Introduction

Golden Fleece is about sheep: how they think (insofar as it is possible for any human being to determine that), and how they act; how their own rhythms and those of range sheep raising determine the patterns of ranch life; the economics of the sheep business. It is also about the people who raise sheep: woolgrowers, that is, ranch owners; shearing crews, ranch hands, and herders; and those who, like Hughie Call, find themselves suddenly a part of ranch life.

Hughie Florence Dickinson Call was a fourth-generation Texan, brought up in flat, urban land. She was born in 1890, eldest child in a doctor's large family. By her late twenties, she had done some professional writing and was a widow with a young son. Thomas J. Call, twelve years her senior, moved to Montana from his native Kansas in about 1893 and took up breaking horses in the area around Dillon. Sometime before 1914, he became the active partner in a firm that bought a home ranch, purchased and leased land from homesteaders, and obtained government allotments in order to raise sheep in the Madison Valley of southwestern Montana, eighteen miles south of the town of Ennis. The death of his first wife in 1909 had left him only parent to a baby son who was taken to live with Tom Call's sister in Colorado. Tom Call and Hughie Dickinson met on vacation in California in 1919; they married, and Hughie first came to the valley in the summer of 1920. The sons from their previous marriages, Leigh Call and Andy Dickinson, came to the ranch too and were joined in 1921 by Tom and Hughie's daughter Louise—who lived just until she was sixteen.

Although there were plenty of sheep in Texas, Hughie Call's only experience with lambs before her arrival at the ranch had been, as she put it, with "a leggy creature which skipped about on frosted Christmas cards." Everything about the ranch was unfamiliar— from the road down into the canyon where the home ranch lies (a grade that has not changed over the years and, for all her frightened

ix

reaction to it, is less steep than those on many major western highways) to the rhythm of ranching and the communal life among ranchers and their employees. One of the ways in which Hughie Call coped with her new environment was to write: first articles based on particularly humorous episodes in her early years on the ranch, then books. Several chapters of *Golden Fleece* originally appeared in magazines. Two books for children and two more for adults followed it.

The Little Kingdom is about the Calls' daughter and her short life on the ranch—a subject only briefly touched on in *Golden Fleece*. *Rising Arrow* and *Peter's Moose* are about boys much the age Andy Dickinson and Leigh Call were when Tom and Hughie married. *The Shorn Lamb*—a novel with a predictable romantic plot—is about a young widow trying to run a ranch on her own; one cannot help speculating on how much of it may stem from the author's own sense of always being a tenderfoot, never quite belonging in the ranching community. All five books contain much detail about ranching life, interwoven because, as the reader of *Golden Fleece* soon learns, the life of the ranch is totally inseparable from the life of those on the ranch.[1]

There are some gaps in Hughie Call's story. The reader who wonders about the impact of the Taylor Grazing Act of 1934 on the Call ranch must take into account that Tom Call used Forest Service allotments, not Grazing Service and Bureau of Land Management lands, and was thus unaffected by that landmark legislation. Nor does Tom Call seem to have been active in Montana's powerful livestockmen's organizations. The power of woolgrowers in Montana was suggested in an 1892 federal report on the industry, which noted that the sheep business in Montana was "a State industry in fact, and any legislation necessary for its protection or encouragement is readily secured. In consequence of these favorable conditions, the sheepmen, who are much abused in many other States, are here leading citizens and [wear] the most prosperous dress of farmers and stockmen."[2] Tom Call was a member of the Montana legislature when he remarried—a fact unmentioned in *Golden Fleece*—but his name does not appear on published membership lists of the Montana Wool Growers Association. While a few of Tom's neighboring ranchers appear in *Golden Fleece*, they are present chiefly as amused observers of his wife's attempts to adjust to Montana ranch life. Little attention is paid to their working together except in such practical matters as cutting ice and shipping lambs to Chicago markets.

However, the story is not really Tom Call's; it is Hughie's. She notes that a Montana rancher rarely gives advice straight out; a story is used to convey a message, and one has to read between the lines to understand. Hughie Call's story is more straightforward than the ranchers' often were; read through, it is an informative as well as entertaining account of just how the sheep business works. There is in it no sense of detached observation. While some of the people on the ranch seemed very strange to Hughie (and some of them *were* very strange), they are portrayed as partners in the enterprise all of whom were vital to the ranch community—as she found herself to be. Tom Call is always present as manager of the ranch and its people, though the reader does not get to know him very well as a person. Other sources suggest his success and his impact on the people around him.[3]

Some parts of the Calls' story as told in *Golden Fleece* are oddly misleading. Tom Call's earlier marriage is not mentioned, nor is Hughie's. Although her own son simply appears in the story, Tom's is depicted as having been born during their marriage. Stories of Leigh Call's babyhood are inventions or modifications that the author devised to make a point about her own life. At least one member of Hughie's family, a much younger sister, lived on the ranch for some time, but her observations are not included. Still, neither the isolation in *Golden Fleece* of the Calls' experiences nor some changes in details of family life reduce the value of the book. In its organization it is an impressionistic picture of sheep-ranch life; in its details, it is a careful account of the problems and pleasures of that life as lived between 1920 and 1942.

Not all participants were committed to such an existence. Having spent their youth on the ranch, Leigh Call and Andy Dickinson chose not to be sheep ranchers. In 1944, Tom and Hughie sold their ranch to a local group and moved to southern California. Tom Call, who had not been well even before the sale, died in Pasadena in 1946. Hughie then moved first to Missouri (where she taught creative writing for a time at Drury College) and then back to Texas. She often returned to the Madison Valley during the summers, and her comings and goings were reported in the Great Falls, Virginia City, and Dillon newspapers with considerable pride. The tender-

foot's efforts to convey her own new world had obviously set well
with long-time residents. In 1966 Trinity University in San
Antonio—which she had attended when it was the San Antonio
Female College—gave her its Distinguished Alumni Award. She
was the first woman to be so honored. Hughie Call died in 1969 in
Texas and was buried next to her husband and daughter in the quiet
little cemetery just outside Ennis.

Meanwhile, the ranch underwent changes. It was sold again in
1948, this time to a New Jersey realty company whose president
moved his family west to live on the ranch. They and the intervening
owners ran only cattle on the ranch's eighteen thousand deeded acres
and twelve thousand acres of forest allotments. In 1965, the old
ranch house that at first had so unnerved Hughie burned down. A
modern house a bit farther down the canyon of Wigwam Creek has
replaced it. The ranch outbuildings—including the big log barn—
and the corrals are still there, although not all the structures in
outlying areas have survived. Nothing has come to spoil the view
from the ranch of the abrupt and jagged Spanish Peaks to the east
and south, nor of the timbered, domed Gravelly Range to the west
up Wigwam Canyon. From the switchbacks a few miles up Call
Road (which understandably becomes Devil's Lane at about 8,200
feet) near the national-forest boundary, a visitor can see almost the
whole of the middle Madison Valley. Its green and gold coloring,
typical of the interior Northwest, suggests both the potential
richness of the country and the hard work required to make it
productive.

The middle Madison Valley has not changed much in general
appearance in the last hundred years. The sheep and cattle that are
the ranchers' prime products are not often visible from the highways
through the valley, and few tourists venture up bumpy, narrow dirt
roads like Call Road. Most visitors come to the valley to fish. In the
summer trout season, there are ten fishermen per mile of river per
day in this part of the valley.[4] One prime fishing spot is Varney
Bridge, the nearest crossing of the Madison to the Call ranch. In the
fall, hunters come to the valley. The ranch of *Golden Fleece*, like many
of its neighbors, is posted and hunting is allowed there only with
written admission. There have been minimal efforts in recent years
to subdivide some of the ranch lands in the valley. A very few

modern houses—some garish, most obviously not working residences—have been built along the edges of the mountain ranges so their owners can enjoy the views across the valley.

The first white settlers in this part of the valley overflowed from Alder Gulch—soon to be Virginia City, still county seat of Madison County—in the late 1860s. Like many who made money from mining, they settled and raised food for the miners across the Gravelly Range. The land they worked was hardly prime agricultural land: the old, broad river valley is covered with rocks and less than eighteen inches of precipitation falls each year. Nor has there ever been much effort at mining in the valley. Nonetheless, the area grew. Ennis, the largest town in this part of the Madison Valley, was soon on the route of three freight roads and two stage lines.

Predecessors to Tom Call's sheep were brought to the valley early. By 1868 there were over 1,700 in the county—a third of the sheep in Montana then. Rams for breeding came from the east, but ewes were trailed from Oregon, California, Idaho, and Utah. In 1891, shortly after Montana became a state, there were at least a million and a half sheep in the state and almost 13,000 in Madison County.[5] An 1888 issue of the *Montana Wool Grower* reported that five million dollars was invested in Montana sheep; the wool clip in 1876 had been ten thousand pounds, that of 1883, four million.[6]

At the turn of the century there were over four and a half million sheep in Montana, and three years later a record 5,736,000 grazed on the ranges of the state. When Hughie and Tom Call were married, there were less than half that many, although the industry picked up enough by 1930 to record almost four million sheep again. In the census years from 1900 to 1930, Montana ranked first, second, fifth, and third in the United States in sheep raising (and has maintained high ranking since). While Madison County—something over twice the size of the valley and its bordering ranges—was no longer one of the major sheep-raising counties statistically, it reflected the same kind of growth: one set of figures shows 13,991 sheep in the county in 1880, 27,275 in 1890, 119,955 in 1900, 128,552 in 1910, and 115,238 in 1920. Up to 1890 there were more cattle than sheep in the county; in 1910 and 1920 there were approximately three times as many sheep as cattle.[7]

As *Golden Fleece* makes clear, sheep raising has never been an easy business or a particularly stable source of income. While sheep can graze in summer on high, rough country—land that cattle cannot use effectively—the inaccessibility of such summer range is a problem in itself. The care of sheep requires many hands: each band of some 1,000 to 1,200 ewes must have a herder, and the herders must receive supplies regularly no matter what the weather or how far from the ranch headquarters he may be. At critical seasons of the year, breeding, lambing, and shearing, a large amount of manpower is needed to accomplish the necessary tasks expertly and efficiently. Tom Call's 14,000 sheep required fifty-three regular hands plus the shearing crews. Prices for wool and lamb are enormously volatile. Bad weather, or a sheep with an odd idea in her head that leads to the pile-up of a band, can spell disaster. So can declining interest in woolen clothing or a downturn in the market for lamb. While Tom Call was an active rancher, per-pound prices for wool ranged from a World War I high of fifty-eight cents in 1918 to a Depression low of nine cents in 1932. [8] With the Depression, too, came federal agencies often too big and too distant to take into account the need for rapid decisions on loans and marketing if the rancher were to survive.

Since the Calls gave up the ranch, sheep raising has become less difficult in some ways, more so in others. Lambs are mostly range-fed rather than fattened in feedlots like cattle. The land they feed on (at least that in private hands) is likely to have been mortgaged regularly to provide capital for the ranch they belong to. For many sheepmen, modern ranching is possible only because the increasing value of land—a five- to ten-fold increase in the past twenty years—gives them something to mortgage. Even in 1960, a rancher who got twenty-five cents a pound for his lamb could make money. By 1980, he required sixty to seventy cents a pound; hay for winter feeding cost seventy-five dollars a ton; prices for mechanized vehicles had skyrocketed, as had fuel costs; and the rancher who preferred to use a well-trained team of horses in his work would find that one costing five hundred dollars in 1960 would sell for five thousand dollars twenty years later. [9]

What is more, the modern rancher is in a constant struggle with the land. He may own eighteen thousand acres—as Tom Call did—but he is likely to use far more than that. Much of it is federal, under the management of the Forest Service or the Bureau of Land

Management. He is allotted a certain amount of that public land on the basis of so many animals per unit of land per month of use, and he pays a grazing fee for the use of the allotment. Over the years, improper use of the public lands and inadequate attention to restoration of prime grazing lands have become serious problems in many parts of the public domain. A good working relationship between ranchers and local Forest Service and BLM staff is critical to solving those problems.[10]

Tom Call ranched before some of these problems became acute, although in many ways he was ahead of his time—especially in his use of mechanization. One early photograph shows him in a 1914 "work car" on the ranch, and he took that car into places where good horsemen might well hesitate to take their saddle horses.[11] The Calls' life was made easier by ready access to a rail line for supplies and for shipping lamb and wool to market; even in the middle of the twentieth century, many Montana sheep ranchers had to trail their lambs great distances to shipping points on the railroads.[12] But a rancher of 1980 has the great advantage of four-wheel-drive vehicles to cover rugged terrain. A decline in sheep production has in some respects made it easier to run sheep: ranges are less crowded, and the highest, most rugged country does not have to be used. Although mechanization has reduced the manpower required to run a ranch, the number of sheep per band and per herder has remained relatively constant. There are losses as well as gains in a modernized sheep business, however: the lore of *Golden Fleece* is all the more valuable because of increased reliance on foreign help, for there is less handing down of lore about sheep and sheep raising from herder to herder.[13]

Despite modernization and vastly increased costs, in many ways life on the ranches has changed little in the past hundred years— much less in the sixty years since Hughie Call arrived in the Madison Valley. Montana sheepmen reported in 1892, at the beginning of the boom in sheep raising in the interior Northwest, that the chief advantages of running sheep there were the atmosphere of Montana, the quantity and quality of available range, and the availability of water. The greatest disadvantages were the expense and the "competence" of herders (who were paid perhaps forty dollars a month and room and board), the isolation of sheep-ranching life, a lack of lumber for ranch construction in some parts of the state, and the rough winters. A 1 percent loss to predators was not among the greatest problems. Eighty years later, Montana sheepmen reported similar problems: predators, prices, weather, disease, lambing complications, parasites, and inadequate help. Only some 37 percent of those who had run sheep in Montana during the preceding decade still did so by 1972.[14]

In 1978, a gathering of sheepmen and environmentalists from the interior Northwest shared further discouraging statistics. In many ways, the sheepmen spoke as survivors—albeit they saw an increasing number of young people coming back to the business. They reported that in ten years there had been a decline of 5½ percent per year in the number of sheep in the country and of about 2½ percent per year in the number of "sheep operators." Not only were there just a quarter of the sheep in the country that there had been at the end of World War II; national consumption of wool was a quarter of what it had been thirty years before.[15]

Nevertheless, sheep ranchers are optimistic. Perhaps they have reason to be. The increased cost of corn and grain fed to livestock makes the primarily range-fed lamb a relatively less costly source of protein. The virtues of running both sheep and cattle, past attitudes notwithstanding, may encourage more ranchers to produce both—as is happening aain in the middle Madison Valley. For the first time since the Calls sold the ranch, there is a sheep wagon— shiny aluminum now, instead of canvas and wood—tucked into the folds of its hills. Nearby is a band of sheep. The ranch's present owners lambed 1,200 ewes in the spring of 1980, the first range lambs for years in the valley. Some of their neighbors thought them a bit crazy to raise sheep, others envied them. The sheep did fine, and their owners understand very well why Hughie Call's life was so controlled by the animals'.

Notes

1. *Rising Arrow* and *Peter's Moose* were published by the Viking Press, New York, in 1955 and 1961, respectively. *The Little Kingdom* and *The Shorn Lamb* were issued by the Houghton Mifflin Company of Boston (the original publisher of *Golden Fleece*) in 1964 and 1969.

2. H. A. Heath, "The Sheep Industry in Montana, and North and South Dakota," in *Special Report on the History and Present Condition of the Sheep Industry of the United States* (Washington, D.C.: Government Printing Office, 1892). p. 701.

3. Leigh N. Call, "The Call Ranch," in *Pioneer Trails and Trials: Madison County, 1863–1920* (Virginia City, Mont.: Madison County History Association, 1977), pp. 772–73.

4. Charles E. Brooks, *The Living River* (Garden City, N.Y.: Doubleday & Co., 1979), p. 129.

5. Heath, "Sheep Industry," p. 717. The figures were provided for tax purposes, and Heath's own estimate is that there were about 2,000,000 sheep in the state.

6. Montana Writers Project Files, Livestock Study, Montana State College, Bozeman (microfilm, Montana Historical Society, Helena), reel 23, p. 517; *Montana Wool Grower* 5, no. 5 (December 1888): 67. Toward the end of the Depression, in 1938, there were less than twice as many sheep in the state, but they were worth nineteen million dollars. *Montana Wool Growers News Letter* 12, no. 3 (March, 1938): 21.

7. Edward Norris Wentworth, *America's Sheep Trails: History, Personalities* (Ames: Iowa State College Press, 1948), p. 307; Montana Writers Project Files, Livestock Study, reel 2, n.p.

8. Data compiled by the Montana Wool Co-operative Marketing Association, reported in "Montana Fiftieth Anniversary Edition," p. 5B, unidentified clipping dated July 4, 1939, Montana Historical Society.

9. John T. Peavey, telephone interview, September 8, 1980.

10. Ibid.

11. Leigh N. Call, "The Call Ranch," p. 773.

12. Wentworth, *America's Sheep Trails*, p. 306.

13. Peavey, interview.

14. Heath, "Sheep Industry," p. 714–15; Kenneth Seyler, "Primary Conditions Affecting the Montana Sheep-Raising Industry," multilith, Brands-Enforcement Division, Department of Livestock, State of Montana, Helena, February 14, 1973, pp. 3, 5, 45.

15. *Proceedings of the Conference between Environmentalists and Sheep Producers, Sun Valley, Idaho, September 1978* (Helena: Northern Rockies Action Group, 1979), pp. 7, 18, 19, 41, 45.

Contents

· I

It made a good story

I HAVE been trying for more than twenty-five years to live down the name of Tenderfoot. I remember looking up the word when I first came to Montana, because I was curious to know just how long a sentence I must serve before I could hope to be eased into the fold of the initiated. The definition, *a newcomer in a comparatively new or unsettled region*, left much to the imagination, and I placed my own construction on the words. Being a supreme optimist, I concluded that once I had put down roots I should automatically acquire the status of native.

I was wrong. There may be sections of Montana where this miracle could take place, but not in the Madison

Valley. There is no middle ground here. You were born in the Valley, knowing those things you should know, or you move in and are supposed to know only the things you are told. If you listen and never ask stupid questions, you're a wise tenderfoot. If you talk when you should be listening, you lay yourself open to a kindly, tolerant ridicule that sticks to you the rest of your days.

Early blunders brand you and, since Valley memories are uncomfortably good, these blunders crop up when you least expect them. My first makes a good story to this day.

I was born and reared in a Texas city, and until I married a sheepman and came to live in Montana, I had never seen a range of mountains, I had never seen a snowstorm or a chinook, and a lamb meant nothing more to me than a leggy creature which skipped about on frosted Christmas cards.

I had been a sheep rancher's wife less than a week when a careless herder let his sheep stray into an alfalfa field, with the result that a dozen or more ewes bloated and died. Tom (my husband, also known as 'the Boss') was very angry and sent the camp-tender up to bring the offender in. The herder was a small wizened Mexican. I could not but feel sorry for him when he was told, after five minutes of sound abuse, to roll his bed and get down the road. The moment he left the room I protested indignantly.

'That's downright inhuman! He's far too little to carry a bed.'

Tom was already figuring the herder's 'time' on the back of an envelope. He's a man of few words, but he has a ready smile, and he grinned without looking up from his column of figures. The camp-tender, who stood waiting for the herder's check, hastened to reassure me. 'That Mex is tougher than he looks. He'll manage all right.'

I was still incredulous and walked over to a window which gave a good view of the bunkhouse. My vigil was rewarded presently, for the herder emerged with only a small canvas-covered roll on his back. I turned about gleefully. 'He's left his bed and I don't blame him a bit!'

The camp-tender moved over to the window. ''Tain't much of a bed,' he admitted, 'but he's taking it with him.'

If I had only stopped then, but I didn't. 'His mattress and bedstead and springs — he hasn't got them.'

The camp-tender stared, and suddenly his face was convulsed with an effort to conceal his mirth. He tried to say something, choked on the words, and made a dive for the door.

Tom was not so considerate. He threw back his head and roared with laughter. A moment elapsed before he could explain that a sheepherder's bed consisted of several blankets and a heavy, square comfort known as a 'soogan' rolled up in a canvas tarp.

I laughed then. I thought it was funny too, but later it ceased to amuse me. No fire ever spread over a forest more rapidly than that story spread over the valley. I can laugh about it now, but just the same I never tell a herder that his ewes have wintered well that I do not watch for a betraying gleam of laughter in his eyes, that I do not sense the inner workings of his mind: *How can she tell if a ewe has wintered well or not? She didn't know a bed-roll when she saw one.*

Nevertheless, there are advantages to being the kind of tenderfoot I was. When you've acquired the reputation for abysmal ignorance, you can sink no lower. All you need do is to settle yourself as comfortably as possible on the hard bedrock and listen and learn. You don't have to ask questions because, with a foresight that is positively uncanny, your neighbors, and even the men employed on your ranch, will beat you to them. They explain everything down to the last intricate detail and they keep on explaining. Their patience has its roots in kindliness, and only a half-wit could fail to soak up some of the knowledge.

2

The land of shining mountains

WE LIVE near that part of Montana which is known as the
cradle of Montana history. Just over one of the lofty
mountain ranges that flank the Valley lies the historic town
of Virginia City, scene of the Alder Gulch gold rush. In
the sixties Virginia City was a lawless flamboyant metropo-
lis of thirty thousand inhabitants. Today, it is difficult to
remember that its quiet streets ever resounded to the tread
of miners and freighters, road agents and bawdy women.
For Virginia City is almost a ghost town now, with a popu-
lation of scarcely three hundred people.

The first woolgrowers who settled in this Valley came out
by wagon train to Virginia City when the gold rush was at

its height. They turned their backs on Alder Gulch, where fortunes were made overnight, and guided their weary ox-teams up a tortuous mountain trail and then down into the fertile valley of the Madison River.

Those first woolgrowers were men of rare vision. In hectic, glamorous days when the chimera of gold still had its grip on the land, they weren't deluded. They sought a business that would endure — one they could put their faith in and cling to the rest of their lives. Their foresight and wisdom was rewarded, for I know a number of ranches in this country which are owned and operated, and have been continuously, by the children and grandchildren of those same steadfast souls who staked their all in a strange new land.

Those early settlers seemed to share one taste in common. Almost without exception they built their cabins in canyons or sheltered coulees. What they lost in perspective they gained in protection from the bitter, snow-laden winds. Of course they still got the wind from two directions, but at that their troubles were halved.

It has been said that the wind in the Madison Valley blows four ways at once, and I could almost believe it. At any rate, in the course of a blizzard I've seen the wind change direction several times in less than an hour, sweeping over exposed land like a gigantic broom and, as the storm gathered force, hurling great chunks of snow aloft, to rest at last against fences and other obstructions. The snow piles up inch by inch around sheltered canyon ranches but it seldom drifts, while the ranch houses built on hillsides or flats by a generation less canny than the pioneers are lucky not to be half-buried in snow before the winter is over.

I have one friend whose house sits out in the middle of a

level stretch of land. It is lovely in summer because she has an unobstructed view of the entire valley. For the rest of the year she has my sympathy. Every time she leaves the house to feed chickens or gather eggs, she is forced to climb over great drifts which completely cover her gate and fence. She never gets daylight through two of her kitchen windows because hard-crusted drifts are packed from the ground to the low-pitched eaves of her roof. These shut off the view from late fall until spring, when the chinook winds melt them away. She told me once with a wry little smile that her husband no longer attempted to keep the drifts shoveled, as he had when they first built their house. He was, she said, no match for the wind, which replaced the snow almost as fast as he could shovel.

At Stonyacres, the home ranch buildings are set down in a canyon. Tom bought this particular section of the ranch thirty years ago from an Old-Timer who, because of illness, was forced to retire. When Tom decided to build, he moved the Old-Timer's cabin several hundred feet away and erected our present house on its site. Curiously enough, we have no feeling of being shut in here. The topography of our canyon is rather unusual. We're protected from the wind and we still have a view.

Wigwam Canyon, so called from a creek of the same name which flows through its length, is shaped much like an arrowhead. One end narrows to a mere slit, no wider than the willow-bordered creek bed, but the gradual slope of the canyon walls permits a spectacular view of the snow-peaked Gallatin Mountains, one of the most beautiful ranges of the Montana Rockies.

The other end of the canyon is much closer to the house, less than three miles, in fact, and it spreads out fanwise through cliffs of rose-colored rock. Gnarled old cotton-

woods, black birch and quaking aspen follow the course of
the creek from this direction to its source, and in the gap
between the widespread walls the mountains seem to
interlace, the edge of one fitted behind the edge of another
as far as the eye can see.

So long as I live, the approach to the house from the big
red gate on the county road will never lose its charm for
me. I shall always see it as I saw it that first day, always
recapture that sense of wonder and delight.

Tom had told me that his ranch house was down in a
canyon and this interested me no end, for I had never seen
a canyon. I began looking for it the moment we drove
through the big red gate. For perhaps a mile and a quarter
the land rose steeply and then it flattened out into fertile
hayfields. I scarcely saw these hayfields, for beyond there
sprawled a long range of timbered mountains, whose towering beauty held my eyes. I forgot to look for the canyon,
forgot everything but the wonder of those distant, shining
peaks.

There was not one sign of life or habitation, no houses or
barns — not even any fences. Suddenly I experienced a
curious sense of isolation, a complete apartness from the
present-day world; as though Tom were not beside me; as
though I had started out alone on a long journey which
would not end until the road slipped over those distant
shining peaks into the mystery of the other side.

I should not have been surprised to see a herd of buffalo
come thundering toward me pursued by painted befeathered
Indians. It was strange that this thought occurred to me,
for less than a century ago the Indians did roam these very
hills and mountains. We never plow up new ground that
we do not uncover hundreds of arrowheads. At the foot
of one of the rose-colored cliffs south of the house, Indians

camped for long intervals in a bygone day, chipping out obsidian arrowheads and hunting big game. Their tepee stones still pattern the land above the cliff, and at its base we have collected many discarded, imperfect arrow points, as well as specimens of obsidian. So numerous are these Indian relics that I have even found them while weeding a perennial flower bed which runs along the creek near the house.

Tom broke the silence abruptly now. 'Look. We're coming to the canyon.' His words jerked me back to the present and I stared. We were on the brink of the canyon, and there had been not one sign to indicate its nearness. The car dipped and began to creep down a steep narrow grade, so steep and narrow that my heart skipped a beat and my toes curled up in my oxfords.

Five hundred feet below I saw the white, red-roofed, tree-encircled buildings of my new home. Ranch sounds, which carried distinctly in the clear mountain air, rose up to greet us — the bark of a dog, a barn door squeaking on rusty hinges, the clank of an anvil in the blacksmith shop and then the deep mellow tones of a bell. The last notes echoed softly down the canyon — thin, silver threads of sound. . . . 'It's like something you hear in a dream,' I said. 'Too lovely for words.'

Tom grinned and speeded up the car.

'No dream,' he replied, bringing me down to earth with a jolt, 'but lovely all right. That's the "wash-up" bell. Dinner in half an hour and I can take it. I'm hungry!'

3

The home ranch

A MOMENT later we were driving through a gate at the foot of the hill and into a barnyard. We passed a number of buildings which Tom pointed out as barn, blacksmith shop, granary and two implement sheds. Beyond the big log barn there were several corrals, but the mechanics of ranching did not hold my interest that morning. I was looking for the house; disappointed and a little impatient because a windbreak of giant cottonwoods screened it from view.

I was to learn that the windbreak worked two ways, for it screened the straggling buildings of the barnyard and the adjacent corrals just as effectively from the other side of the creek. Many times since I've been grateful for this.

I'm quite sure the Old-Timer who planted the cottonwoods would scoff at such squeamishness. No doubt he was proud of his barnyard and grudgingly set out the trees because the Homestead Law of that day required that he do so in order to prove up on his land. Whatever his motive, he did me a favor.

We came to a gap in the windbreak and here a small bridge spanned the creek. Overhead the cottonwoods interlaced, forming a graceful arch; sunlight sifted through their branches and danced along the water.

Along the bank near the bridge a robin paused in his task of extracting a worm from the earth, cocked his head on one side and regarded us with bright, inquisitive eyes. And then we drew up before the house.

'Well, here we are,' Tom said. 'Welcome home.'

Home. I looked at the house. I saw it was large, sturdy, with several chimneys on its roof, and many gleaming windows. All one could ask for, and yet — something was missing, something was wrong. A moment elapsed before I realized what that something was, and then wave after wave of homesickness swept over me.

The house stood out in stark silhouette against a background of mountains — strange, unfriendly mountains they now seemed — without one flower or shrub or blade of grass to soften its austerity.

Living in Texas I had always taken flowers and green things for granted. I had not even thought to ask Tom if there was a lawn about his ranch house, and he had considered the lack of so little importance that he failed to mention it, as he failed to mention a number of things for the same reason.

I climbed slowly out of the car and waited beside the gate while Tom unloaded our bags. For a long, dreadful moment I stared at the ground surrounding the house. I had never before seen so many rocks in one place. Big rocks and little rocks, a veritable carpet of them. Here and there I saw a clump of gray-green sagebrush which had put down roots in a handful of earth, but that was all. The rest was rocks.

I ached to protest, to say I couldn't stand it, but one glance at Tom left me mute and helpless. His face wore a proud, pleased expression. I could not spoil that moment of homecoming for him — nor other moments either, it seemed, because two months elapsed before I got up the courage to discuss the planting of a lawn. But I never forgot; it was always in the foreground of my mind, never budging, crowding the other problems which continually harassed me.

We started up the gravel walk. I had given scant attention to the house, but now, as I looked at its four-square walls, I became suddenly conscious of another disconcerting fact. This was a man's house. Its very architecture proclaimed the fact that no woman had helped to plan it. There was no nonsense about it; no useless shutters to rattle and bang in the wind, no dormer windows to hold the drifting snow, and no decorative intricacy of roof line. You knew from its look that the walls were thick and the windows snug and tight. (So tight, in fact, that I had lived with them several winters before I could open one unaided. Tom still regrets the moment of weakness which resulted in his planing them down for my convenience. He grumbles frequently that wind comes in around the sashes, that it has taken more wood for heat ever since.)

There was one concession to beauty that I failed to appreciate that day, a broad veranda which ran along the front and one side of the house. I could not know that wild clematis vines, dug up the canyon and transplanted by me, would soon climb riotously over its roof and lend softness and charm to the boxlike proportions of my home.

The veranda was a lucky accident, I later learned. When the house was built an error in calculation resulted in the contractor's having too much lumber on his hands. I still marvel that he could have persuaded Tom to let him make such use of it, for a veranda in the ranch country of Montana is about as useful as a tattered umbrella in a driving rain. Ranch people have little time to idle on porches before nightfall, and then, even in midsummer it is usually too cold to sit outside in comfort. The moment the sun slips down behind the mountains, the cold creeps in, and the average rancher is much more likely to be toasting his toes before a fire indoors.

Tom opened a door and we entered a small, bare hall. Somewhere I could hear the heartening crackle of a wood fire; the rattle of a pan. Except for that the house was strangely quiet. I had not expected a rousing welcome, but this utter indifference to our arrival, on the part of the cook at least, seemed queer.

I did not know the inviolate code of the ranch kitchen then and Tom didn't think to explain, but I know and approve it now. Nothing short of accident or death must interfere with the cook's schedule; she has no time to chat between the 'wash-up' bell and the serving of a meal; that second bell must ring on the dot, because a delay of even ten minutes represents a loss of five working hours when thirty men are involved.

A stairway led out of the hall and I followed Tom up its uncarpeted steps. Before I had reached the top I knew that the inside of the house was even more masculine than the outside, and it will always be that way. I missed a good chance to add a touch of femininity when I first arrived, and it's too late to do much about it now. I should never have got very far anyway. No mere woman could have strewn knickknacks and nonessentials all over the place. A hard-boiled Amazon, perhaps, but not an easy-going little Texan.

I've changed a lot since Tom showed me over the ten rooms of his house on that day years ago. Many of the things I believed necessary to my welfare and comfort then seem wholly unnecessary, and even useless, now. I should not know what to do with them if, by some miracle, they were suddenly forced upon me. But I'll have to admit that it took me quite a while to reach this state of mind.

I have learned to love the big sunny rooms of my home — their freedom and space. Strange that I could ever have thought them cold and bare and unattractive. And yet I did. With each door Tom flung open for inspection that first day, my heart sank a little lower.

There were five bedrooms — almost as bare as the cells of monks. Each contained a bed, a straight chair and a chest of drawers. There were no curtains, no rugs, no pictures and no mirrors; just stark essentials. And the rooms were as like as five peas in a pod. I remember wondering a trifle wildly if I should ever be able to tell them apart, ever be sure which one was my own.

To each of these rooms, over the years, I have added a mirror, a lamp, a table, a hooked rug and a comfortable chair. There are still no pictures on the walls and no curtains at the windows, but this has ceased to worry me. I do not need pictures on the wall when my windows frame living pictures, whose texture and color — from sunrise to sunset, from season to season — are never the same. Who but a blind man could curtain such loveliness?

There was also a bathroom on the second floor, but it was bath in name only — a cubicle marked up on the plans as such, which Tom had never got around to equipping. He explained unconcernedly that there'd been a little difficulty about the water system, not enough pressure from the spring he'd planned to utilize. He'd work something out eventually. (Eventually? I wondered, remembering that the house had then been built five years.)

'Where do you bathe?' I faltered, staring at the four walls of that empty room.

'Up Wigwam Creek — summers,' he replied. 'In a laundry tub before the kitchen range in winter.'

I tried to conceal my dismay but he sensed it, for he added quickly, 'I'll try to work out some sort of water system after the lambs are shipped.'

After the lambs are shipped. Five words, so pregnant with meaning, so important to me in the years that were to follow. Strange that their meaning did not sink in then. I was to learn that the price the lambs brought had to pay the entire year's ranch expense before the wool money could be spent for luxuries, or even the bare necessities of life.

I was glad to quit that second floor. I believed I had seen the worst, but my first glimpse of the living-room downstairs did not tend to raise my spirits. My eyes traveled slowly over every piece of furniture in the room. That didn't take long because there weren't many pieces.

It was a huge room, and the scanty furnishings and bare windows made it seem even larger. Two sturdy brown-leather chairs and a matching leather lounge, whose stiff tuftings reminded me of an oversized waffle, were lined up against the walls. A round-bellied stove sat forward near the door. A stove — when I had pictured a great fireplace . . . ruddy flames dancing through five-foot logs.

I have since discovered that an open wood fireplace, though pleasant to look at, has about as much chance of repelling Montana cold as the feeble glow of a tallow candle. It lets in more cold than it can possibly offset, and much of the heat escapes through the chimney. Few ranches in our part of the country are even heated with coal-burning furnaces. Coal has to be trucked over a steep mountain range from the nearest railroad and it is very expensive. Wood-burning stoves were then, and still are, the most popular method of heating, because timber is practically at our doors and can be had, in many cases, for the cutting and hauling.

However, there is nothing which can seem so cold and forlorn as an empty, unlit stove. The one I looked at that day had an isinglass front, as bleak and staring as the windows of a deserted house. I could not know how I would come to bless that friendly isinglass; how, on bitter winter evenings when the windows were crusted with ice and the wind howled around the eaves of the house, I should sit for long moments, warm and content, watching the firelight and shadows leap up against that door and play on the wall.

A flat-topped walnut desk took up the space between two of the windows. This was really a fine piece, but my eyes passed it over swiftly, for I had spied something that caught and held my gaze. The pelt of a huge grizzly bear lay stretched out in front of the stove! This glassy-eyed monstrosity, with its wide-flung jaws and wicked teeth, was a little too lifelike for comfort.

'Where did you get that?' I clutched Tom's arm and pointed.

'Old Ginger Foot? I trapped him two miles up the canyon.'

Only two miles? I did not ask for details, but then and

there I placed Old Ginger Foot at the top of a mental list of things I could not live with. My optimism was misplaced, for I walked around the pelt for three years, in fact until Leigh, our first child, began to crawl.

Tom clung jealously to that weatherbeaten pelt. He valued it as he valued no other one possession. When I heard, in detail, the story of the grizzly's wholesale slaughter of sheep, the years it had taken Tom to track the killer down and put an end to his life, I did not have the heart to carry out my plan.

Leigh took care of that. I owe the present rug on my living-room floor to the fact that my son was also passionately attached to Old Ginger Foot. He had chewed off one of its ears and pried out a glass eye before Tom became alarmed, snatched his trophy away and carried it off to the office for safety.

The dinner bell rang and we came through the front hall into the large dining-room beyond. Certainly I could not complain of bareness here. Two big oilcloth-covered tables ran the full length of the room and I counted thirty-two chairs drawn up to these tables. The largest heating stove I'd ever seen dominated one end of the room.

Jennie, the cook, rushed in from the kitchen with two great platters of fried ham, which she deposited noisily on an end of each table. Introductions were brief. Tom said: 'Hello, Jennie. This is my wife.' Jennie flung me a wide, friendly grin and shook hands with 'one foot in the stirrup,' as Tom later described it. Then she was off, returning immediately with two bowls of boiled potatoes. She was actually panting from her exertions before the last of that enormous meal was placed on the tables, and she finished not a moment too soon, for the men began to file in through the door.

I had rather dreaded meeting all those men at one time. I needn't have. Montana ranch men seldom show their emotions. I know they were delighted to see Tom but they greeted him casually, as though he'd only been gone overnight. For my part, when Tom said, 'Boys, this is my wife,' thirty pair of eyes focused in my general direction for a split second and were lowered to the table before I had time to say a word. I fought back an almost irresistible impulse to laugh out loud as the men, ignoring me completely, heaped up their plates and fell to. Throughout that meal not one of them even glanced my way. You would never have guessed that I had been the favorite topic of conversation in the bunkhouse for the best part of a month, as Jennie later assured me I had been.

When lunch was over, Jennie showed me her kitchen. It was small. Too small, I thought, remembering the big kitchen in my Texas home. I had to do the cooking unaided just once to appreciate its convenience. Lined up against the wall on one side were a cabinet, a zinc-covered table and a metal sink. On the other side a great range with an attached reservoir, a bench which held water buckets and a well-filled woodbox. Not one inch of lost space in that kitchen, no necessity for a single needless step. I could stand at the table and balance an egg-beater in a bowl of flapjack batter with one hand while I reached over to the stove and stirred a kettle of oatmeal with the other.

The drainboard of the sink and the zinc-covered table were less than two inches apart. This grouping, I discovered, was a boon for the cook. After each meal the men brought their dishes to the kitchen, scraped what food remained on them into the garbage pail and lined up the dishes neatly on the end of the table. This simple task, which took but a moment of their time, saved the cook many a step. She had no cluttered table to clear up, no remnants of food — only a heart-warming order which, in my case at least, took half the curse off dishwashing.

Dusk had fallen that first day before I discovered that the house was lighted with kerosene lamps. Aside from the fact that it interfered with my reading in the evenings, this did not concern me nearly so much as the lack of a water system. But the water system, it later transpired, could not be had until an electric pump was installed, and that pump was not installed for several years.

The water used in the house in the meanwhile was carried uphill from the creek. Many a time when Tom was away and I'd forgotten to ask the chore boy for extra water for washing or bathing, I've lugged those heavy buckets up what seemed a gentle slope to the eye but assumed the proportions of a mountain to the feet and back before it leveled out at the kitchen door.

Of all the inconveniences connected with the lack of a water system, however, the outside toilet topped the list. Ours was built several hundred feet from the house. It had none of the charm of Chick Sale tradition. No half-moons or stars adorned its door. That toilet was dark and cold in winter and dark and stuffy in summer. Only the Puritan Fathers could have taken its drawbacks with equanimity.

For one thing, it faced the wind coming and going, up and down the canyon. Curiously enough, the wind which whistled through every crack and knothole in winter passed right over the roof in summer. Since all possible ventilation came at the wrong season of the year, I decided it would be a smart idea to shift the cubicle sidewise. Tom didn't agree. He insisted that ventilation, even winter ventilation, was necessary. But Tom was inured to cold. I

wasn't, and the cold in that torture box struck straight
through to my spine.

I remember that there was diversion in the shape of a
Sears-Roebuck catalogue, hung from a nail on a stout cord,
but I never got around to any wishful ordering. I never
dallied that long.

4

Other shoulders turn
the wheel

WHEN I promised to marry Tom, I resolved that I'd learn
to be an efficient ranch wife in the shortest possible time.
I was prepared to work hard and make sacrifices. What sort
of sacrifice was not clear in my mind, but I'd read a good
many books about city girls who married and went to live
on isolated farms and ranches and I was convinced there'd
be plenty.

Tom and I met first while we were both vacationing in
another state. We became engaged and were married in
less than six months. He was then, as he has been ever

since, reticent about his financial affairs. This reticence, I
have learned, has its roots in a decent modesty.

Tom went into the sheep business when he was a mere
lad, starting out with only a few hundred head of ewes
which he paid for with money he had earned when most
boys his age were going to college. He was lucky because
he bought on a falling market. For the several years that
followed, the price of wool and lambs ran high, and he came
out of this cycle of prosperity with two bands of sheep
(around three thousand head).

He worked hard and put every dollar of his profits back
into the business. When I met him, he was taking his first
vacation in fifteen years. In these years he had bought and
paid for this ranch, section by section, and had built up his
flock to fourteen thousand ewes. He did not tell me the
story of his progress until after our marriage, and then I
had to dig it out of him bit by bit.

Our backgrounds were even more widely divergent than
either of us guessed at the time. Tom had come up the
hard way and I the easy. He was generous to a fault, but
he thought of money in terms of so many hours of toil. He
never ran a bill unless cash was in sight to pay it. When
his funds ran low, he did without.

I was the eldest of a large, happy-go-lucky family. My
father, a doctor of the old school, had a fine practice, but
unfortunately he also had a fine sensitivity where money
was concerned. He could never have dunned a patient for
an unpaid bill, consequently his income was only about
half what it should have been.

We lived well on that half — too well, in fact, for not one
of us had any conception of the value of money. Money
was something to be spent as long as it lasted, and when it
was gone we lived on the same scale until more could come

in. It always did. The years I've spent in Montana have taught me to look facts in the face. I know now that we lived far beyond our means; that we frequently mortgaged our future. Such a statement would have shocked my parents profoundly, but it is true, nevertheless.

Of course, Tom and I discussed our future life together in the brief time we had, but our discussions covered very little ground. In the main, they consisted of the problems which might confront us because of our different upbringings. Tom was worried for fear I'd be lonely and unhappy without the diversions of a city. I felt sure I could make this adjustment, but I was disturbed lest my ignorance of ranch life and lack of practical experience might work a hardship on Tom. I believed he needed an efficient wife, one who could carry her share of the load. I did not reach this conclusion from anything he said, but rather from the things he failed to say.

One would have to know Tom to understand his reticence. It is a part of him, as ingrained and deep-rooted as his wisdom and honesty. I, on the other hand, am an extrovert, and like most Southerners, *I tell all*. My life, my ambitions, my finances and my problems are an open book to anyone I'm fond of. I'm quite sure I left nothing unsaid, and Tom left a lot.

He had told me that his vacation was enforced. A stubborn cold, which developed into pneumonia, lowered his resistance. Convalescence was slow and his doctor ordered him off to a warmer climate until he should be fit for work again. His concern over the way his business was run in his absence, and his anxiety to return to the ranch, led me to believe that his whole future was threatened. My vivid imagination pictured a small ranch, inadequately manned, and desperately needing the physical help of its owner.

Small wonder that I was totally unprepared for the size of the ranch and the number of livestock run there. It was a little disconcerting, in view of my noble resolutions. I was ready and eager to put my shoulder to the wheel, but I had about as much chance of horning in on that wheel as a London slavey might have had of crashing the Court of Saint James's. Other shoulders, more capable than mine, were already turning it smoothly. I experienced the curious ineptness of a man who has braced his strength to lift a sack of cement, only to find a sack of feathers in his hands. Everybody on the place, save me, had jobs to do that occupied each hour of a working day which began at sunrise and ended at dusk. Nobody had time to invent tasks for a clumsy outsider.

I should have saved myself a lot of needless fretting and loneliness had I discussed the matter honestly with Tom, had I said at once that I must have something to do. But I hated to bother him. He was so preoccupied, so terribly busy. His vacation over, he hurled himself into his business with the dynamic energy and enthusiasm which had brought him thus far.

He was seldom home. All day long he rode about in his car supervising ranch activities — the preparation for haying, the moving of sheep and the building of a new lambing shed at one of the places on the ranch known as Cherry Creek. I rode with him quite a bit until I had been over every acre of the ranch, but there were many days when it was not convenient to have me along, and those days were strangely empty. I wanted so to be in the midst of things — to be of use — and I didn't know how.

Jennie refused my proffered help, telling me frankly that she was accustomed to working alone, that it disturbed and upset her schedule to have another woman in the kitchen. Looking back, I'm sure this was only a half-truth. I was too eager to learn the routine of the kitchen and Jenny was canny. She wasn't teaching me anything that might endanger her job.

She did teach me to wash. I had to learn, for laundresses were practically nonexistent in the ranch country of Montana at the time. Jennie had been doing the house laundry and Tom's as well, but it was not in the bargain that she should take on mine. I was a willing pupil and before the summer was over had offered to do Tom's laundry too. I didn't know what I was letting myself in for until winter came. I remember my shock and dismay the first time I tried to take a suit of long underwear off the line. It had ballooned and frozen into a grotesque, unmanageable shape which wouldn't bend. I can still see myself, plowing through snow on tiptoe, holding that rigid underwear as high as my arms could reach.

But I welcomed washday throughout that first summer because it left me with a feeling of accomplishment. The rest of the time I rattled about in that big house like one seed in a gourd waiting for the evenings when Tom would be home. For the first time in my life I couldn't read; I couldn't concentrate that long. I could not even talk intelligently because nothing was straight in my mind.

The size of the ranch confused me, there were so many points of activity on those thousands of acres of land. Certain things were done at this place, others at that — all Greek to a newcomer. I suppose these things seemed so simple, so perfectly obvious, that nobody went into the customary detail which would have cleared up matters for me.

The questions I asked in those days — the answers that tripped me up and left my brain a scramble of disconnected geography and data! I was breaking the ground for my reputation of tenderfoot when I insisted upon knowing all about the different camps — their reason for being and their proximity to the ranch, as well as the specific duties of the men who worked for Tom. I tried to learn too many things at once and it couldn't be done. After the first week I began jotting down my impressions and the things I learned, as I learned them, in a small notebook. I began to get some place then.

Six months ago I ran across this book again. I had not thought of it for years. I'm not given to self-pity, but as I leafed slowly through its many scribbled pages I found time to feel sorry for the bewildered little greenhorn who made those notes. I wanted to laugh and cry at once. It all came back so vividly — the way I checked and double-checked to make sure my data were right, the hours I spent memorizing things my children knew soon after they could talk! It did not seem possible that anyone could have known so little about ranching or livestock or sectional geography.

A crude miniature map covered the first page. I had painstakingly copied this map from a large one of the ranch properties which hung on the wall of Tom's office.

Next I had listed the various places on the ranch:

Home Ranch: On Wigwam Creek, at extreme northern boundary of the ranch. Headquarters. All supplies kept here — grain, cottonseed cake, corn, salt, as well as groceries for herders. All alfalfa and grain harvested here. Buildings: House, bunkhouse, barn, four 120 × 40 feet sheds, blacksmith shop, granary, icehouse, one cabin and chickenhouse.

Cherry Creek: Twelve miles south of home ranch. Lambing camp. Native hay irrigated and put up here. Buildings: Cookshack, bunkhouse, barn and three large sheds.

Sunrise Creek: Ten miles south of home ranch. Shearing sheds (used also for lambing earlier in the spring). Buildings: Cookshack, bunkhouse and two large sheds.

Arthur Place: (Bought from a homesteader and still called by his name.) Ten miles southwest from home ranch. Buildings: Cookshack, two lambing sheds, barn and bunkhouse.

Tate Place: (Also bought from a homesteader, etc.) Seven miles southwest from home ranch. Buildings: cabin and one lambing shed.

(I shall have to admit that these were merely the salient facts. The rest described in detail the way the shadows fell on this mountain or that, the way the spruce trees bent to the wind, the ruffled, golden edges of a cloud at sunset, a herd of antelope grazing on some distant grassy slope or wild geese skimming through the sky.) The National Forest came next. I had not yet been to the Forest when these notes were made, hence the description was sketchy.

National Forest Reserve: Southwest and adjoining the ranch. Owned by the United States Government, which sells grazing to woolgrowers at a cost of from six to ten cents per head of sheep for the summer season. All sheepmen in this vicinity have specified allotments which they use year after year. Headquarters camp, from which herders are supplied, on each allotment. Tom's allotment is thirty-five miles *straight up* from home ranch. Steep road, barely a trail. Supplies taken in by pack train.

From there I went on to the duties of the various ranch men and I had got the scenery out of my system, for these notes were to the point.

Herders: Eight of them. They live in compact little wagons for the months their sheep are grazing on the ranch, and prepare their own meals. To get inside wagons you have to step on wagon tongue and climb through door. Bunk is crosswise at far end of wagon. Enclosed bench, with hinged top, runs from door to bunk on one side. On other, a sheet-iron cookstove, with cupboard close by. A shorter bench extends from this cupboard to bunk. Adjustable wall table lets down across bench as needed. Space under benches and bunk for supplies and herder's belongings.

Camp-tender: Visits each sheep camp once a week and moves camp to new grazing area when necessary. Supplies herders with groceries, tobacco, dry wood, water and sheep salt. Takes care of herders' personal business — mail, money orders, etc. Checks boundary fences and reports condition of sheep and range to Tom.

Chore Boy: Called chore boy, but must be over forty. Milks cows, separates milk and churns, cares for garden and chickens, splits kindling and keeps woodboxes filled, carries water and pinch hits, in emergencies, all over the ranch.

Irrigators: Two of these. They irrigate alfalfa and grain here at the home ranch, and later the native hay at Cherry Creek. They get up before daybreak and ride horseback to fields, where they change water. Return for breakfast and go back, taking a lunch with them. Get in for supper but always late. Change water again after supper and sometimes work until ten oclock.

Hay-diggers: Called this because they dig (pitch) hay in the field. Twenty-two of them here now. Tom says two more when they start stacking.

Trucksters: Two. Truck cottonseed cake and corn (in carload lots) from the railroad. Groceries from wholesale grocery in Butte. Wool, as it is sheared, from shearing pens to railroad warehouse. Rams, during breeding season, to different herds of range ewes.

Here and there, as I turned page after page I smiled over certain notations — recalling how strange or amazing they had seemed to me then, how taken for granted now:

There are sixty-two miles of fence about this ranch!

Tom buys his flour and sugar by the ton and his coffee, beans, rice and dried fruit by the hundred pounds. Buys canned goods in dozen-case lots. Cellar looks like the warehouse of a wholesale grocery.

Have not heard a single man 'mister' Tom since I came. They call him Tom or the Boss. Seems cheeky to me. Don't see how he keeps their respect, but he does. Jennie calls him the Boss or HE, and I'm the Missus or 'She' to all of them.

They think I'm going 'high-brow' when I speak of the noon meal as lunch. I can't get used to calling lunch dinner and the evening meal supper. They differ in name and time only. Both are huge meals. The men seldom talk at table. They march in solemnly, slide into their seats and fall to. They stack their dishes when through, get up and stalk out. Afraid I was responsible for this silence but Jennie says not. She approves of the silence — it gives her more chance to talk!

They even work on Sunday here.

They worked on Sunday, and I had so little to do that I was driven to describing the ranch and its activities in a notebook. But I didn't feel guilty as I closed the small dog-eared book and tucked it away in my desk, for I was busy on Sundays too before the next summer was over. And never since has any day seemed half long enough.

During the eight years which followed I fitted into the traditional pattern of the Montana woolgrower's wife, learning that Tom and I were secure, that our children, three in that time — Leigh, Andrew, and Louise — were secure only so long as the sheep were well cared for; learning that neglect or carelessness in the pursuance of even my own small part in the scheme of things could well become a boomerang, which struck back at the ones I loved best, and threatened their welfare and happiness.

5

We name the ranch and
plant a lawn

BACK in those days few of the ranches in this valley had names. They were known as the Thayer Ranch, the Jeffers Ranch or the Wiles Ranch as the case might be and this suited the owners, but it bothered me.

'Why don't you call this ranch something?' I asked Tom one morning.

'Call it what?' he countered, definitely not interested.

'Some name that will fit the land. Let — me see ——'

He refused to take me seriously. I know now that Tom **was** secretly dismayed. In spite of his modesty, his pride was involved. He had built up this ranch acre by acre into something which closely resembled a small kingdom and he had done it alone. It was a symbol really — won by years of back-breaking toil and stark sacrifice. The ranch was known as the Call Ranch, which was right and proper. Instead of explaining all this, he put me off by suggesting outlandish names — Woolly Acres or the Baa-Baa. So the subject was shelved for a time because I could think of nothing suitable and he would not cooperate.

Some days later Tom had to go out on his range to look over the grazing and I went with him. We followed no trail or road. The grass was high and the sagebrush thick. Unluckily the rocks were thick as well. We hung the car up on a great boulder concealed in the grass and knocked a hole in the crankcase. We could drive no farther and we were all of seven miles from the ranch.

As we reluctantly set out on foot Tom asked me with a grimace, 'About that name for the ranch — how would Rockyacres do? Or Stonyacres?'

'*Stonyacres.*' I turned it over in my mind and liked it very much. 'That's perfect,' I said.

I was simple enough to expect his approval and disappointed when, instead, he dryly related the story of a farmer who years ago had called his small, barren tract of land 'Sagebrush.' It had tickled the fancy of his neighbors and thereafter the man was known as 'Sagebrush Murphy.'

I have learned since that the old-time Montanan seldom gives advice. He will tell some story that illustrates his point and let it go at that. You're supposed to catch the point and profit by it. If you don't, more often than not you'll be sorry. For instance, he would never tell a newcomer on the sort of pleasant, starlit night which is sure to follow a storm that his car will freeze up if he leaves it outside. He'll say: 'Pretty night. Don't think I've seen so many stars out in a year. Not since the night Jeff Wade's radiator froze up and busted.' The newcomer is then expected to announce that he has anti-freeze in his radiator, or that he thinks he'll put his car under shed.

Tom's story of 'Sagebrush Murphy' was meant as a warning but it passed completely over my head. I was even then deciding the proper type and size of lettering for a sign I planned to hang over the gate.

The next morning I told Jennie we had named the ranch and here, too, I failed to arouse any enthusiasm.

'Don't you like it?' I asked.

'I guess it's all right,' she replied gloomily, 'but it'll make strangers think there's no grass anywhere on the ranch, and the Boss has some of the best range in this valley.'

I met with discouragement elsewhere. A week later I drove to a neighboring ranch to return a call. This ranch was owned by a peppery old gentleman who was quite a character in the Valley. Mr. Thayer, a grizzled veteran sheepman with forty lambings to his credit, was uncomfortably outspoken. He disapproved of me, and remembering the occasion of our first disagreement, I hoped I'd find only his wife and daughters at home.

Earlier that summer Mr. Thayer had stopped by our ranch for dinner one day. Throughout the meal he and Tom had discussed the lamb market and in the course of the conversation he said: 'I think I'll hold my black-face cross-bred lambs as long as I can. There's a big demand and the price is bound to go up because there's a shortage. Oh, they got some down in Texas and California, but they can't compete with ours.'

I didn't like the way he said it and my dander was up.

'That's queer,' I remarked with thinly veiled sarcasm. 'I happen to know that Texas leads in sheep production.' (I hadn't known until Tom told me.)

Mr. Thayer turned his grizzled head toward me. I think he saw me for the first time and I had the feeling that he didn't like what he saw. The laugh wrinkles smoothed out of his face, leaving it as blank as a schoolboy's slate that has been wiped clean with a sponge. Today I would be warned that I was stepping on hallowed ground, but I didn't know it then.

He informed me in a cold, stiff voice that it was quality that counted, not quantity. That Montana lambs raised in the mountains took on a sound, hard fat that a lamb raised in lower altitude could not hope to equal.

I caught Tom's eye. He shook his head violently and put a finger to his lips, but I refused to take warning. 'The climate is better in Texas,' I defended. 'You'll have to admit that.'

'Better!' the old gentleman snorted. 'God A'mighty, woman, don't you know it's *cold* that makes good wool?'

Better, not *more*. That day I learned the code of the Montana woolgrower, the ultimate end toward which he toils. Long before Mr. Thayer was through with me I felt as a blowsy ragweed must feel when it springs up in a bed of lilies. I knew when I was licked.

Unluckily Mr. Thayer had to be home the afternoon I've mentioned. His presence took the fine edge off of my enthusiasm but presently I did tell Mrs. Thayer and her daughters that we were going to call the ranch Stony-acres. They liked the name — were keenly interested. I said, 'Why don't you name your ranch?'

'Why don't we?' one of the Thayer girls replied. 'Let's do it.' Thereupon we began to discuss appropriate names.

The head of the house was sitting near a window reading his paper. He didn't take part in the conversation but I noticed that he began to fidget in his chair.

'Somehow, I always liked Indian names,' Mrs. Thayer said wistfully. 'I was raised on a ranch near the Big Horn River. I wonder how Big Horn Ranch would do?'

'Now, Ma, that's silly,' her eldest daughter discouraged. 'We don't live on the Big Horn River. We don't even raise cattle.'

'I know we don't.' Mrs. Thayer was about to discard the idea when her face lighted up. 'Some rams have horns, though!' she exclaimed. 'We could nail a pair of ram horns over our gate. That would make it all right.'

She got no further. Her husband crumpled his paper and threw it from him. He leaped to his feet. To this good day I can still see the horrified expression which spread across his apoplectic face. It was not enough that his good friend Tom had married an outsider. She must come up from the South with a lot of new-fangled notions and sow the seed of discontent in the hearts of his 'wimmen-folks.'

'Oh, no, you don't!' he bellowed, shaking a gnarled finger at me. 'Tom can go by the name of Stonyacres Call for the rest of his life if he's a mind to, but I'll be damned if I'm going to be called "Big Horn Thayer."' And with that he stalked abruptly from the room.

I saw the light then, and I'll have to admit that I began to have a few misgivings of my own. I needn't have. I started something. It wasn't long before most of the ranches around us were given names, and a joke can cease to be a joke when it becomes a boomerang. Mr. Thayer won up to a point, however. His ranch got a name — but it wasn't Big Horn.

Innocently enough I antagonized Mr. Thayer again that summer, but I did not learn that I had for a year.

In middle August I asked Tom to plant a lawn about the house. I remember approaching the subject diplomatically, careful not to give the impression that there was one thing about my new home that did not seem perfect to me. 'I'd like to look after a lawn and a flower garden,' I told him. 'I haven't enough to do.'

I'd better have taken off my gloves at the start. He believed me and suggested that I might try raising pheasants to fill in the time. 'You couldn't take care of a lawn,' he explained. 'It would have to be irrigated from the big ditch up the canyon.'

'I could learn to irrigate, couldn't I?' For weeks I had been sustained by the thought of that lawn. I could see it slipping away from me.

Tom seldom wastes words when he can make his point in a better way. He took my hand and led me to a place about six hundred feet from the house, where he showed me one of the biggest boulders I had ever seen.

'We dug it out,' he informed me, 'when we excavated for the house. Multiply that rock by twenty and you'll get an idea of what it means to plant a lawn in this country.'

I multiplied and burst into tears. He insisted upon the truth then, and I confessed that I was homesick and not always happy. I should be that way, I told him passionately, so long as I had nothing to look at but rocks. He might have reminded me of the man who could not see the forest for the trees — but he didn't. He was instantly contrite and understanding and promised me a lawn.

With my usual optimism I hoped to have the seed in the ground before winter, for early spring sprouting. But snow flew before the ground had been prepared for planting.

I no longer wondered that there were so few lawns in the mountains. Some of the boulders were so large that it took a four-horse team to drag them off; it took truckload after truckload of dirt to fill up the gaps that were left in the earth. It also took several men out of the hayfields at a most inconvenient time of the year, a factor which then gave me small concern.

I didn't discover for some time that it was not the labor involved, so much as the problem of irrigation, which troubled Tom. Mr. Thayer enlightened me. He stopped by the ranch one day to borrow a piece of farm machinery. I had been watching the chore boy irrigate the new stand of grass about our house and I asked Mr. Thayer proudly what he thought about it.

The light of battle slanted across the old gentleman's eyes, his Adam's apple did alarming gymnastics in his throat and he all but choked on a wad of tobacco.

'Do you know how many acres of alfalfa that water would irrigate?' he hissed.

I shook my head puzzled.

'*Five!* Five good acres of alfalfa! How many ewes do you suppose that hay would winter?' This time he was sure I didn't know anything worth knowing and he didn't wait for a reply. '*Seventy-five!* Seventy-five ewes! And they're not going to eat that hay because somebody got a notion to pretty things up!'

I gasped, and then gathering in the fragments of my scattered dignity said in a stiff voice, 'I can't see how my lawn can possibly be any concern of yours, Mr. Thayer.'

'She can't see how her lawn can be any concern of mine,' he groaned hollowly. 'I'll tell you how. My wimmenfolks has seen it. They've been badgering me for a week. Nothing'll do but they got to have one too. From now on I

got to waste two inches of water every summer on some
good-for-nothing grass that I ain't even allowed to turn a
lamb onto. No, sir! We got to have a picket fence to protect our pretty lawn.'

This verbal chastisement took place the second summer
I spent in Montana. I have never seen Mr. Thayer since
without remembering every word of it. His lawn and tidy
picket fence were mute witnesses of his defeat — a defeat
in which I had played an unwilling leading rôle. I never
felt quite easy in his presence. . . .

I ran across the old gentleman one day last spring. Time
had passed him by. He looked as hale and hardy and bellig-
erent at eighty-three as he had looked at sixty. His truck
was bogged down in a mudhole, a particularly tricky mudhole which ushered in the Montana spring each year as
surely as the bluebird and the meadowlark.

When I drove my car over the top of the hill he was
leaning against a fencepost, but he hurried forward and
gestured me back. I didn't need his warning to know that I
could never pass his truck without encountering difficulties
similar to his own. I'd had the peculiarities of that mudhole
explained to me a hundred or more times over the years,
several times by Mr. Thayer himself.

'There ain't no bottom to it,' he told me after we had
settled ourselves comfortably on my running-board to wait
for his son to return from a near-by ranch with a team.
'The commissioners have dumped enough gravel into it to
pave the road from here to town.'

I agreed with him and then, because I had always found
it hard to converse with Mr. Thayer, I asked the first thing
that popped into my head. 'What were you planning to
haul today?'

'Leaf mold for our lawn,' he replied, an anxious little

wrinkle creeping up about his eyes. 'We had the prettiest lawn in this part of the state till last summer. Then she began to turn yaller in spots. Had a feller out from the college at Bozeman last week to see what we could do to save it. He told us to try leaf mold.'

I stared at him and a hysterical giggle caught in my throat. From his tone one would have supposed that Mr. Thayer had pioneered lawns in the state. My frantic efforts to keep from laughing must have been transparent, for he looked bewildered for a moment, and then the laugh wrinkles began to play about his fine old eyes.

'Damned if you wasn't the one got me into this,' he chuckled, and gave my arm a friendly pat. 'Been meaning to tell you for some time back that I'd quit holding that lawn against you. Fact of the matter, I sort of like it myself!'

But it had taken him more than twenty years to tell me, and all that time I'd had the uncomfortable conviction that Mr. Thayer had about as much use for me as he had for a drought.

6

The rural telephone

ALL the problems of that first summer were problems of adjustment to fixed customs and a way of living foreign to anything I'd known before. I was new and the customs and standards of living were as old as the state itself. I was convinced that I'd have to fit in with the accepted way of living as quickly as possible, but some of the customs were a little more than I could take.

Foremost among these was the habit our neighbors had of 'listening in' on the country telephone line. This practice was general, and its matter-of-fact acceptance was revolting to me. I could scarcely conceal my distaste when anyone related a bit of news in my presence and casually admitted that he'd heard it while listening to a telephone conversation which I felt sure was not meant for his ears.

I can 'listen in' as brazenly as the rest now. It's one of my favorite diversions, but in those days, before my children were born, I could no more have stooped to 'eavesdropping' than I could have tampered with Uncle Sam's mail.

This lack of tolerance and understanding was unfortunate. Had I spent even a small part of my time 'listening in' that first summer I should not have been lonely and I should have been encouraged to learn that other ranch wives had problems which, if not the same, were as hard to iron out as my own. But a lot of water ran under the bridge before I became convinced that there was nothing secret or shameful about 'listening in' and regretted my smugness.

The country telephone is something more than mere wires strung on tall poles, than receivers and mouthpieces. It is a living, vibrant thing which welds the interests and problems of isolated communities in a way that is past understanding.

The telephones are even equipped with a convenience for the eavesdropper — a little gadget on the left side of the instrument which can be released if you want to talk or left in place if you'd rather listen. Thus is quiet ensured. A mother can balance a fretting baby on her hip and get the news without having to worry lest the noise disturb her neighbors.

Many ranch wives do their own work and have only snatches of time between dishwashing and potato-peeling and the cooking and serving of three huge meals a day. They may have a spare moment to listen, but no time to become involved in talk. The country telephone has all the advantages of the radio or the talking machine. It can be turned on or off at will. No danger of your pies burning while you learn the latest local news, for you can leave your post without seeming rude, take a peek at the pies and come back again. You may have missed a little, but you can always catch up if the conversation interests you enough.

I shall never forget my first contact with 'listening in.' I walked into the dining-room one morning to find Jennie leaning indolently against the wall, the receiver glued to her ear. This surprised me. Until that day I had never seen Jennie idle. Ordinarily she whizzed around with a purpose and energy that put me to shame. I was pleased to see her take time off for — I suppose — a chat with a friend.

I had come downstairs to ask some question and I went on into the kitchen to wait until she was through. She didn't get through. Moments elapsed before it dawned on me that Jennie was eavesdropping.

Grim with disapproval, I came back to the dining-room, pulled a chair out from the table and sat down. Jennie might have me bested and on the defensive where ranch work was concerned, but I felt I could teach her a thing or two about ethics and I meant to do it.

I waited and Jennie listened.

The moments ticked on and finally I said, 'Jennie, I'd like to speak to you.' I was not handling this matter well and the knowledge put an edge of sharpness to my voice.

I expected her to drop the receiver sheepishly, but not Jennie. She gestured for silence and listened ten minutes longer. When at last she put the receiver back on its hook and turned about, I was too angry to care what I said and I voiced my distaste in no uncertain terms. Her calm eyes widened with surprise.

'Why, Missus,' she told me, as though conveying a fact I'd be delighted to hear, 'that's all right. Everybody listens. You're supposed to. It's a good thing I did. Ellison's ditch broke and flooded the road for a quarter of a mile. Old man Thayer's stuck down there with a truck full of hogs and Jim Anderson's taking a team to pull him out. He...'

I cut her short and explained with all the patience I could muster that I was not interested in other people's business. I should have said more, but she interrupted excitedly: 'But Missus, it *is* our business. The Boss's trucks was coming that way with cottonseed cake. If they get stuck, it'll take a block and tackle to get them out. I'm going to ring down the line and ask the Thextons to send them up through the field.'

That took a little of the wind out of my sails, but I was still unconvinced and indignant. When she had delivered her message, I warned her that I never wanted to see her 'listening in' again.

She took me literally. I never *saw* her do it, but oh, how she listened! That woman knew everything that happened within a radius of fifty miles and she naïvely regaled the ranch hands at meal time with the gossip. She knew that the Ellisons had sowed their oats before the 'shiftless Burtons' had more than broken their ground. She knew when the Lawtons sold their hogs and what they got for them. She was righteously indignant when the doctor in a near-by town refused to bring the Burton baby into the world, because he hadn't yet been paid for the last five Burton heirs. This story shattered my heroic reserve and I urged Jennie to go right down and see what she could do; I even offered to take her down.

'Grandma Basset'll go. She's the closest.'

'But she may not know about it. It would be criminal to leave that poor woman alone at a time like this!'

She looked me squarely in the eye before she turned back to her work. 'Don't worry,' she said. 'She *knows*.'

She did know. I later learned that Grandma Bassett had taken immediate charge of the Burton affairs, had browbeaten the doctor into making another entry on the debit side of his ledger, and furthermore had stayed with the mother until she was up and about again.

Several months later a lamb buyer telephoned Tom and offered him nine dollars per hundredweight for his lambs. Tom would not commit himself, but promised to think it over. No sooner had he put down the phone than our ring came through. I answered, and a woman's excited voice called over the wire: 'Tell Tom not to take nine dollars for his lambs. I heard that lamb buyer make Jim Anderson the same offer last night and Jim upped him to nine dollars and a quarter.'

I did a sum in mental arithmetic before I replaced the receiver. That message would make Tom some money. Jennie eyed me expectantly as I turned away from the phone, but I took a mean advantage. I refused to relay the message until Tom and I were alone.

These two incidents gave me food for thought, but it took something that struck even closer to bring me into line. Leigh was not quite a year old at the time. Jennie had married a 'dry farmer' and we had a man cook. I wouldn't admit that it was dull without Jennie, for if it was, I knew why. I missed her chatter — and her 'listening in.'

One afternoon during the first lamb drive of the season, the ranch was deserted save for Cy, the cook, my young son and I. Cy adored the baby and spent all his spare time amusing him. I had letters to write, so I left them together on the back porch and went upstairs to my desk. Cy had been peeling green apples, and upon my return I found the baby alone, gurgling gleefully, with his small mouth full of apple peelings. I was frightened, of course, and worried throughout the balance of the afternoon because I couldn't be sure just how many peelings he had swallowed.

By ten o'clock that night I knew he had swallowed too many. He grew restless, cried out repeatedly in his sleep and began to run a temperature. I did everything I knew to do, but my efforts were futile. Around midnight his body began to twitch and draw. I considered calling Cy, but to do so I should have to go to the bunkhouse, some eight hundred yards away, and I dared not leave my son.

Terrified, I sped down the stairs and tried to call the doctor. His wife answered the telephone. She told me he was out in the country, on a maternity case; she doubted if she could get word to him.

'You've got to get word to him!' I gasped. 'I'm all alone, and I'm afraid my baby is having convulsions!'

She assured me she would try, but she didn't sound encouraging. I was frantic with fear, and for a moment I clung shakily to the receiver, wondering if there was anything else I could do. Even now Leigh could die before the doctor got back to town and then drove all those miles to our ranch ... Just as I was on the point of returning the receiver to the hook, a woman's voice called out:

'See here, child, have you any hot water?'

'Yes ... *Yes*.'

'Put your baby into a warm bath right away, and get some cold compresses on his head. Jeff's backing out the car this minute and I'll be with you as soon as I can make it.'

If you've ever been alone, ignorant and helpless, with someone you love slipping away before your eyes, you'll know what that message meant to me. I carried out her instructions, eased the small, rigid body of my son into a

warm bath and placed cold compresses on his head. After
what seemed hours to me, my neighbor arrived.

She took charge with the efficiency that comes of long
practice, while I carried out her orders. We fought shoulder
to shoulder — I, white and shaken and no doubt clumsy and
ineffectual; she, grimly, but very, very surely. Ah, that
woman, that blessed woman. I can hear her now ... 'There,
he's comin' out of it ... Look, his eyes is back natural ...
Now his breathing's easier ... You ain't sick, you onery
rascal. You're just tryin' to scare your poor ma to death.'

When the doctor's car drove up to our door, Leigh was
sleeping quietly and naturally. The doctor assured me that
everything had been done as he himself would have done it.

There are some things you can't thank people for, things
that are too big for words, but I clung to my neighbor's
work-worn hand and did my feeble best. She patted my
shoulder in her friendly fashion and laughed.

'Lord, child, you needn't thank me, just give thanks for
the party line. I knew nobody would be ringing town that
time of night unless they were in trouble. I just naturally
had to get up and listen.'

She didn't think she'd done anything unusual. She'd
have done the same thing for anybody. But I had learned a
lesson. From that time on I 'listened in' brazenly and I
was never dull any more.

One afternoon I overheard a rancher's wife call him in
town and tell him to bring home some bread. They expected the threshers the next day, and she couldn't bake
because something had gone wrong with her yeast. Her
husband was so absent-minded that he was a community
joke, and I worried about that bread until I heard his car
rattling down the hill. It was a mere skeleton — that car.
A box, nailed to a few boards, formed the seat. Nothing

was hidden; even the engine had no hood. If the bread was there I couldn't help but see it, and I rushed out to the yard to have a look. Sure enough, he'd forgotten the bread. Before I had time to think, I found myself running down the road in his wake.

'You've forgotten Bertha's bread!' I shrieked. 'We baked today. You'd better take some of ours.'

The car stopped with a sudden grinding of brakes. He got out and thanked me sheepishly. As I packed the still warm loaves in a box it never occurred to him to ask, 'How did you know that Bertha needed bread?' and it never occurred to me to enlighten him.

Another time, in the busiest part of haying season I overheard a hardware merchant in town telling a rancher that it would take three days to get new teeth for a broken rake. 'Hay-diggers' work against time in this country. The season is so short that every hour counts. I knew that the laying up of a rake for three days was nothing short of a tragedy. We had the same kind of rakes and some extra teeth. I got into my car and took them down to him. He was grateful, but not a whit surprised.

I don't think I ever knew the real meaning of neighborliness until I came to Montana. Ours was a large, closeknit family. We were sufficient unto outselves, and had few contacts with our neighbors. In my home city I sometimes sent flowers when I happened to learn that a neighbor was ill. In this country, with the doctor miles away, illness can assume alarming proportions. You always know about it, via the rural telephone line. You don't send flowers, you *take* an extra hot-water bottle, a bag of ice or a change of bed linen. Sometimes the only help you can give is releasing a worried mother from the kitchen, for ranch work must go on, illness or no. But whatever there is to do, you do it gladly, knowing full well that when trouble strikes, the same will be done for you.

I never complain now when I'm trying desperately to hear over long distance, although every receiver that goes down weakens the telephone circuit more and more. I just yell a little louder.

I'll have to confess that there are times when I wish I had the courage of a Forest Ranger in our district. There was a rumor abroad that the Government intended lowering grazing fees on the Forest, and this was a matter of vital importance to every sheepman on the line. All the receivers were down and it became increasingly harder for the Ranger to hear. Presently he could no longer hear. Patience exhausted, he slammed the receiver down on the hook and gave the general ring.

'Listen, folks,' he begged, 'I can't make head nor tail of what the supervisor says unless you hang up. Do it as a favor to me and when I'm through talking, I'll ring back and tell you what he says!'

He didn't keep his word, though, and I've always had a grudge against him. I had to learn the Government's decision from a neighbor who was 'on to him' and wasn't taking a chance on missing a single thing.

7

Sheep bought it

A RANCH wife raised in the sheep country has the advantage. She already knows that there's nothing too good for a sheep. This the tenderfoot has to learn, and the sooner she learns it the better for all concerned. If she takes over her duties in the summer months, as I did, the chances are good that she may retain her self-esteem until fall. She won't have to compete with the sheep because at this season they should be grazing on the National Forest. And the word *compete* expresses it poorly since the sheep always come out on top.

Several summers ago I met the young bride of a local sheepman. She was a charming Eastern girl, apparently very sure of herself and her ability to cope with any situation. Her enthusiasm was contagious. The country was wonderful, her husband's ranch perfect (or would be when she got around to making a few changes), and her husband — well, he was the most wonderful, the most considerate man on earth.

'He'd give me the moon, if I wanted it hard enough,' she confided, her vivid face alight with happiness.

Maybe he would, I reflected, ready as usual to hope for the best, and in this case having a lucky break. So far as I knew sheep had no use for the moon.

I wondered about that little bride a good many times as the months went by, but a year passed before I saw her again. We met in town at the blacksmith shop one day, and while we waited for our separate machinery repairs, I tried to talk to her. She was very reserved and the sparkle in her young eyes had given way to a look of strained bewilderment. I knew what lay behind that look and I longed to reassure her. But I could hardly rush up to a stranger, who had not given me her confidence, and say:

'You'll like it again after a while. You'll get used to being less important than a sheep. You won't mind waiting for things; never getting to go anywhere the day you planned; always going the next day or the next... Try to see the funny side of this crazy situation while you're making your adjustments and don't let the sheep get you down. You'll surely be sunk if you do.'

Driving back to the ranch, remembering my own experiences, I was sorry I hadn't talked to her frankly. One incident in particular I wished I had told her, and later I did.

This incident was significant because it gave me a first inkling of what I had to expect. It took place in September of my first year in Montana. We were shipping lambs and

I was driving with Tom in the wake of one band of four thousand confused and badly frightened lambs. Three days before they had been cut away from their mothers on the Forest Reserve. They had come peaceably enough over forty miles of rough mountainous country to which they were accustomed, but when the highway, some fifteen miles from the shipping point, was reached, it took all the skill and patience of four men and several dogs to keep them moving. Passing cars, driven by impatient motorists, kept splitting the band, and this can come to be a serious matter if it isn't taken care of promptly.

The lead of the lambs pressed close to the bellwether, but a bunch which had been separated from the rest hung back stubbornly and refused to budge. Tom honked his horn again and again, hoping to frighten them into action; the herders frantically rattled their 'tin dogs' (a string of cans on a wire that made an ungodly noise); the dogs raced and barked — to no avail.

It became evident after a while that three balky lambs in the lead of the bunch were causing the delay. A balky horse or mule isn't in the same class with a balky lamb. He plants his four legs squarely on the ground and there he stays. If he stays long enough, every lamb in his wake becomes obsessed with the same notion.

Before long Tom's patience was exhausted. He climbed out of the car, swung open the door and pitched the trouble-makers one by one into the tonneau. It was a new car, a shining, plush-upholstered one, and I, of course, protested vigorously.

'Sheep! In this car? You must be crazy.'

'Sheep bought it,' he informed me briefly and climbed back under the wheel.

The incident impressed and amused me so much that I

repeated it several days later to the wife of a neighboring sheepman. She had been a Billings schoolteacher twenty years before. Now she was stoop-shouldered and weather-beaten. She stopped peeling potatoes into an enormous kettle, and for a moment gazed at me with pity in her eyes.

'That,' she informed me grimly, 'won't seem funny to you a few years from now.'

'But it *is* funny, terribly funny. You've mislaid your bump of humor if you can't see it.'

'Bump of humor!' she snorted, going back to her task. 'Twenty years on a sheep ranch would put a dent in any woman's bump of humor. You're no tougher than the rest of us; you just wait and see! You'll learn.'

I did learn what she meant. The sheep people of this country build their lives around the sheep. Sheep grow best in isolated areas, so the ranches are widely separated. But were the distance between ranches lessened, the isolation would still remain — for half of the year at least.

Our roads are drifted in and often impassable for weeks on end. A trip to town represents unbelievable hardships if a blizzard is blowing. Before a car can attempt the journey, snowplows must clear the road of huge drifts, which invariably blow in again before the return trip can be accomplished. It sometimes takes from six to eight hours to clear the road for only a few short miles.

When the thermometer is hovering around forty below zero, when the fury of the storm is full in your face, when your very breath is whipped from your mouth by the wind and the salt tears freeze up in little beads about your eyes, a trip to town, or even to a neighboring ranch, is something to be reckoned with.

My first Montana Christmas was celebrated the day after New Year, because I had stupidly put off holiday shopping

until the roads drifted in. Tom warned me — as much as
he ever warned me. Early in November he suggested that
it might be a good idea to go to Butte and do my shopping.
I put him off because I was anxious to see a play which was
advertised to appear in a Butte theatre sometime in December. I thought I'd kill two birds with one stone, and I killed
them, all right — in reverse — for I didn't see that play
and I did no Christmas shopping.

Two days before we hoped to leave a blizzard swept the
Valley. For three days it blew and when its force was
spent, we were snowbound. I had no gifts for Tom, the
cook or the ranch men. Our Christmas box from Texas was
in the post office, fifteen miles away, and there it would
stay until we could dig our way to it.

Tom didn't mind for himself; it wasn't the first Christmas
he had missed, but he was sorry for me. Two weeks before,
I had bought some tree ornaments at the drugstore in our
nearest town. Tom insisted that we at least set up and trim
a tree. This was a mistake. Each time I looked at those
gaudy tinseled branches, a lonely red-and-gold box reproached me. True to the custom of the country, Tom had
done his shopping early. This experience taught me a lesson
I never forgot. . . .

But minor tragedies sink into insignificance when compared with an aching tooth that needs the attention of a
dentist, or a stubborn cold that only the doctor can ease.
You can grin and bear until the weather moderates if you
have an aching tooth. You can only pray that you won't
need the doctor. If you should need him the chances are
good that you will have time to recover or die before he
can come to your aid.

I remember an occasion when one of our friends was
threatened with pneumonia. The doctor was called in the

morning; he got there at night. He started out in a car, was met with a sled, and took the last lap of the journey on horseback. The crisis was passed, and the rancher was comfortable before the doctor arrived. As a matter of fact the doctor was more spent than his patient when he finally stumbled through the door.

If you're pregnant you never take chances. You get out at least two months before a winter confinement is due. My children were born in the spring and fall, so I was not confronted with this problem, but one friend of mine was not so lucky. Her experience has etched itself upon my memory.

At the time I first knew her she was the devoted mother of a large family, ranging in years from sixteen to a baby in arms. It didn't take me long to decide that the third young-est child, a little girl of six, was her favorite. The knowledge shocked me, and when I knew the mother well enough, I accused her.

She got up and looked out the door to make sure that none of the children were listening, and then she said hesi-tantly: 'Will you think I'm an unnatural mother if I admit that you've spoken the truth? You see, the rest of the children belong to both of us. But Helen' — her eyes lighted up and for the moment her cares slipped away — '*Helen belongs to me!* She came when I was alone — no doctor, no nurse — not even my husband. I can't help feeling the way I do.'

She told me the story then. She and her husband had been hard put to it to make expenses in those days. Their family had come so fast that there had never been time to catch up financially from one baby to another. They had one band of sheep but these were mortgaged. Each year they had hoped to retire the mortgage, but were never able to do so. They had cut down their overhead as much as they dared; there was but one man in their employ and he was a herder. All the rest of the ranch chores my friend and her husband managed somehow between them.

When she discovered that there was another baby on the way, she was heartsick and rebellious. 'I didn't want Helen,' she told me, with an edge of remorse in her voice. 'It was too much...She was due in February...I knew Bill would make me go into town. All the money we had saved toward clearing the sheep would have to go for hospital bills and the wages of a woman to care for the family in my absence.' Her words trailed off and she sat silent for a moment, looking down at her hands.

Briefly, she forgot I was there. I knew she was living over that time — the hopelessness, the bitter disappointment. She was no longer my vital, active friend — this quiet, patient stranger. I was glad when she straightened her shoulders, smiled and went on.

She had kept her secret from her husband as long as she could. 'Bill already had more than he could do alone,' she explained. 'I was sure he would never let me help with the outdoor chores — feeding the stock and milking — once he knew.'

But the time came when she could no longer hide her condition. 'Bill tried to comfort me, he pretended he was glad. But I knew better. Several times I had seen his face when he thought he was alone...I begged him to let me take a chance; to let me have the baby here. But he wouldn't agree; I had to give in.'

On the day she was to have left home, her husband got word that his herder was suffering from an attack of lumbago and was unable to leave his wagon. They talked it over. The man had had similar attacks and had recovered in less than a week. A few days' delay in reaching town would scarcely matter, it was decided, and so my neighbor's husband set out for his sheep camp. Before he left he piled wood high on the back porch and filled the water buckets. He also warned his wife to turn the calves in with the cows; not to attempt the milking in his absence.

By late afternoon, my friend decided that it would be a sinful waste to neglect the milking. The cream check represented a good share of the family income and she could not bear the thought of wasting anything, under the circumstances.

She milked ten cows and it was dusk before she was through. As she started up the kitchen steps with two heavy pails of milk, she lost her footing, fell and struck her side. She was alarmed until the pain subsided and then, believing she had suffered no ill effects, she went about her duties as usual.

A storm had been brewing all day, and before she got the children to bed, a blizzard began to blow. All night the blizzard howled around the house. She was restless and unable to sleep. Toward morning, when she had just dozed off for the first time, she was awakened by a terrific pain in her side. When the pain grew steadily worse she stumbled over to the telephone to summon help.

The telephone was dead. The fury of the storm, she later learned, had broken the wire only a few yards from the house. My friend was alone except for the children, five miles from her nearest neighbor, and, having given birth to four other children, she knew the fifth was on the way.

She didn't lose her head, but made her meager preparations between spasms of pain that left her weak and dizzy. She heated a kettle of water and put it on the floor beside the bed; pulled up a table to hold scissors, string, towels, a basin and even clothes for the baby. She stoked the fires and finished not a minute too soon; for her knees gave way and she crawled into bed. Half an hour later Helen was born. My neighbor dragged herself erect, and cut the cord and tied it. Then she bathed and dressed her baby girl.

That took high courage and a stout heart. It also took complete understanding. The thing that impressed me most was this: Not once while my friend related her story did she criticize or seem to blame her husband. Her only concern was that I should not fail to see why her small daughter, Helen, stood for something special in her life.

But all ranch wives are not so considerate of their husbands' problems. I know of another woman who divorced her husband for less. They had been married only a year when their first baby came. She was the type of woman who was easily frightened and inclined to magnify her ills. They had no telephone and twice, the week before the baby arrived, she had called her husband from his work and sent him hastily to a neighbor's telephone to summon the doctor. Both times the doctor made that long trip for nothing.

The husband was very busy irrigating his grain at the time. He was unable to stay in the house. It was agreed that she should ring the dinner bell as a signal when the pains again returned. One morning she did ring the bell and he set out immediately to telephone the doctor.

As he drove through his alfalfa field he discovered that four of his ewes had broken through the fence. If he left them to graze until his return, he felt sure they would bloat and die, so he took time to drive them out and prop up the fence.

When he got back to the ranch his wife was in hard labor. The clumsy, terrified husband was compelled to deliver his wife, and the baby arrived just fifteen minutes before the doctor drove up to the door. Those fifteen minutes were the husband's undoing. Beside himself with remorse, he confessed to the doctor that he had stopped on his way to the telephone. The wife was too sick to think about it then, but she remembered it later. It didn't take her long to figure out that the fifteen minutes he had dallied in the alfalfa represented the difference between having her baby decently or *any-which-way*, and she brooded over it.

I liked the husband too. He was a hard-working, inarticulate man. When she told me she intended to file for divorce, I was sure he would never plead his own cause and I tried my best to dissuade her. It was a waste of time and effort. She said flatly: 'It's no use, because I could never forgive him as long as I live. I've had to take a back seat for sheep ever since we've been married. I stood that, but when he risked my life to save *four sheep*, I knew I'd had enough.'

Few of us have been put to such rigid tests of loyalty as the two women I've just mentioned, but all woolgrowers' wives and families have to take a back seat for the sheep. It isn't always easy to accept a situation that seemingly puts your welfare and comfort below that of an animal which is generally conceded to be just plain 'dumb.' I used to hate it; I used to grind my teeth in silent, helpless rage. (I don't exactly cheer about it yet.)

I remember one occasion, during a storm, when our larder was very low (due to my own forgetfulness). We had been out of such staples as baking powder and sugar for a week, and all that time I had been urging Tom to make an effort to get into town. He insisted that the roads were impassable, that it would be folly to attempt the trip until the storm had subsided, and I was reluctantly forced to believe him.

When the storm reached its height, it was discovered that the last sack of sheep salt had been used. Then things began to hum. Within an hour a snowplow and two trucks were bucking the road to town. It was perfectly all right and natural for us to do without sugar, but the sheep must have a balanced diet, blizzard or no!

As I watched those trucks crawl inch by inch up the hill beside the house, I remembered my neighbor's words, 'Twenty years on a sheep ranch would put a dent in any woman's bump of humor,' and I've thought of them many times since. Looking back over the years I've decided that my bump of humor must be cast iron, because I can still laugh.

8

Breeding

THE four major activities of the sheep business usher in the changing seasons. Our ewes are bred in winter, lambed in spring, sheared in mid-summer, and our lamb crop is shipped to Chicago market in early fall.

The sheepman's year begins in November or December with the breeding of the ewes. There are two methods of lambing in Montana — known as 'shed' and 'range.' The ewes which are shed-lambed are bred in November for April lambing. The snow still lies on the ground at this season and the winds are raw and cold. Young lambs would perish if they were not sheltered for the first week or ten days of their lives.

The ewes which are lambed on the range are bred in December for May lambing. The weather is milder in May and green grass has begun to crop up through a thin layer of snow. Occasionally a severe snowstorm necessitates the use of protective sheds, but these spring storms are infrequent and seldom last longer than a few days. We raise only range lambs at Stonyacres, and so our breeding season begins on the first day of December.

We prepare for winter with the single-minded fervor of the squirrel. Soon after shipping, before the frost and wind have stripped the leaves from the trees, we start hauling groceries, corn, cottonseed cake and salt. For whatever needs to be brought over the mountains into the Valley must be hauled before the roads are drifted with snow.

The autumn months are busy ones. As soon as the groceries and feed are stored away in cellar and granaries the winter's supply of wood must be felled. The logs are cut while the weather is good, but cannot be snaked out of the timber until the snow is deep enough to hold the runners of the sleds which haul them to the woodlot at the home ranch.

It takes an unbelievable amount of wood to stoke the stoves at Stonyacres — to heat the house, bunkhouses and all the herder's wagons. The task of bringing the logs in, cutting, splitting and stacking them should be disposed of before the breeding season gets under way.

It is winter in Montana now. The calendar on my desk tells me that the date is November 20, but I do not need this reminder to know that winter has come to stay.

This morning I looked out of my bedroom window on the first heavy snow of the season. Yesterday the high-flung branches of the cottonwood windbreak along the creek were stark and bare against a sullen, leaden sky. Today the sky is brilliant crystalline blue and the naked branches of those same cottonwoods are traced with a filigree of white. Several inches of snow rest lightly on the telephone and power lines, like broad satin ribbons strung out in the sunshine, and virgin carpet is spread over the land.

But I knew it had stormed in the night. My ears are attuned to winter sounds now. When I heard the peculiar muffled tone of the rising bell at five-thirty, I felt sure it was shrouded in white. And later, as I hastily dressed for breakfast, the metallic jingle of log chains, coming from the barnyard, convinced me that this was the storm we'd been waiting for. Today the snow was deep enough to hold the runners of the sleds and the men were making ready to go into the mountain for the wood.

In a week, barring accident, the logs will be stacked in the woodlot, and soon after the air will resound to the drone of a power saw and the ring of axes. One morning I shall look out between the branches of the cottonwoods and see a sight that would be a revelation to the average city dweller — a towering woodpile which is at least seventy-five feet high and fifty feet wide.

It is always a relief to have the wood out of the way before the breeding season begins, for breeding is an all-hand job. This surprised me at first. I had no idea that ewes were bred methodically to lamb on a certain date.

Jennie explained all this to me in patient detail, but even so I'm quite sure the extent of my ignorance escaped her. I can imagine her surprise and amusement had I confessed the truth: that I supposed the lambs all came at once because the ewes were so constituted that they could only conceive in certain intervals — as a bitch dog conceives. I've always been grateful because Jennie did not then, or even after, learn my secret. I was ashamed of my lack of biological knowledge and supposed I was the only adult alive who could possibly have been so stupid. I believed this for years, until, in fact, a cousin visited us during lambing quite recently. This kinswoman of mine was a highly intelligent woman who successfully conducted a business of her own, but she knew very little about ranching and less about sheep.

When she expressed a desire to see something of lambing I took her out to a drop band (ewes to be lambed) and we spent an hour witnessing many strange and intricate phases of lambing. As we were driving home she remarked in an awed voice: 'I had no idea there was so much detail to lambing. Isn't it convenient that the lambs all happen to come at once? I can think of nothing worse than having a job like that strung out over the year.'

I felt like saying 'Thank you' as I forced back a smile and explained that this was hardly a happenstance — that the rams were run separately from the ewes, and only thrown into their bands in certain seasons.

I've never liked rams. I doubt if anyone does except the woolgrower. As a rule he likes them for their market value, which is three times that of a ewe. Tom is proud of his rams. They're a cross of Rambouillet and Cotswold. When bred to a white-face ewe they will produce a lamb which is especially desirable for restocking the herd. The ewe from this cross will grow around three pounds more wool than the black-face ewe, and her span of life is also several years longer.

But just the same our rams are a thorn in Tom's side. Since we run only range sheep, the ewes are bred in rough mountainous country. The rams, three to each one hundred ewes, have to be hauled out to the various camps in trucks, and are left there five days, when the trucks return with a fresh lot, taking the first rams to the home ranch to be rested and fed. Throughout the month of December this same procedure is repeated every fifth day in each separate herd of ewes.

The weather is uncertain and the snow may be deep and

drifted. The blizzards are often fierce and of several days' duration. It's a red-letter day if the trucks succeed in reaching a herd without the aid of a shovel.

The breeding season adds to the herder's troubles too. The rams are not so easily herded as the ewes. They are far more adventurous and lack herd instinct at all times, but are at their worst in the breeding season. Throughout November they have been penned up at the home ranch to be conditioned and fed. When they are eventually turned loose in the herd, they take advantage of their newly acquired freedom. Rams have a maddening way of setting out on independent excursions, and each time a bunch of besotted ewes are sure to follow.

Except for the breeding season and the month which precedes it, most of the rams in this part of the country are herded together. No woolgrower has a full band (fifteen hundred to eighteen hundred) of his own, and it is the custom for sheepmen to combine, turn their rams together and share the expense of the 'buck herd,' as it is called. The buck herder has quite a job. If herders were organized I feel sure the labor unions would insist that a buck herder receive double pay, and I doubt if any sheepman would contest the justice of this increased wage scale.

A ram is slippery. He has just one idea in his head, and that is to break out of the herd and roam the countryside. He's constantly on the alert and never overlooks the possibilities of a sagging gate, a loose fence wire or a post that needs resetting. And if he finds an outlet, makes his escape and wanders into a neighbor's flock at the wrong season, his owner is in for trouble. He can make up his mind to follow the custom and pay for out-of-season lambs, or he can prepare to defend himself in a court of law.

I think I began to dislike rams the second summer I lived

in Montana. Tom was away from home at the time. When the buck herder sent word that a number of rams had broken through a wire fence and that twenty of the runaways were ours, I was not particularly alarmed. Lost sheep, by then, were no novelty to me, and I could not understand the startled looks and sudden burst of activity when I passed the word on to the men. But I understood before Tom's return. Not one day passed that I did not have to placate some irate sheepman on the telephone or in person — but mostly in person.

Those rams did a thorough job. Every last one of them made a bee-line for the National Forest, where approximately seventy-five bands of sheep are grazed in summer. Eventually, after days of riding, our men picked up the runaways in nine different ewe bands belonging to various neighbors. The lamb crop from this unlucky expedition was excellent, but lambs dropped in January cannot survive the cold of the range, and Tom was forced to pay the market price at shipping time for all of them.

9

Good shepherds

THE men were looking for a wool sack. I heard six drawers open and shut. The cellar door slammed twice. Finally they dragged a ladder under the trap door of the attic. I know it was a wool sack they found, because I heard the camp-tender tell the chore boy, as they lumbered down the steps together, that the attic was a *helluva* place to keep wool sacks if you asked him. (I had thought it was a good place when I cached it there last spring.)

I also gathered that the camp-tender wanted the wool sack for a herder's mattress. The wool sack is as versatile as it is popular. It can be used for a mattress, when stuffed with straw, a saddle blanket, a meat sack or an irrigation dam. It might also have been used as the foundation for a hooked rug if I had taken the precaution to lock it in a trunk.

I want that wool sack badly, but there's no use to dash down and claim it now. I could put up a fight and cow any member of this outfit into returning my lawful property, but I can't handle the camp-tender. He knows my weakness for herders and takes advantage of it. If that herder needs a mattress, he needs it, and that's that.

Tom shares my weakness to a certain point. He is pleased to see me hand over the last can of corn or the last jug of syrup because the camp-tender forgot we were 'out'; but he isn't so pleased when he misses his favorite pair of overshoes, mittens or the current issue of a magazine in which he is reading a serial.

He has no recourse. It is understood on this ranch that while the 'Missus' merely accepts, of necessity, the fact that the sheep come first, she's a stern defender of their herder's rights. Not that it ever gets her anywhere. The herders still prefer a calling down from the Boss to a word of praise from the 'Missus.'

The herder is a strange person. (Tom calls this statement a piece of colossal conceit. Why, asks he, is a herder strange? Because he doesn't like women?) I have known two types of herders, and both believe this is a man's world. The first because he knows too little about women, and the second because he knows too much.

The first, a bachelor by choice, reluctantly admits that woman is a necessary cog in the usual scheme of things, but not in his scheme. He boasts that he can best any woman in her own field. He can cook, sew, scrub and clean, and he can do all this in a tenth the time, with a fourth the fuss and effort.

The second has been unpleasantly involved in marriage at some time or other, and has kicked over the traces and taken to the hills. In spite of his disillusionment, he misses the comforts of home. He usually does his housekeeping grudgingly, in hit-or-miss fashion. He values his isolation for obvious reasons, but he is pathetically grateful for a loaf of home-baked bread or a bucket of doughnuts or cookies.

It is well to sort the herders into their separate types as soon as they come on the job. Once I lost a cook during threshing because I neglected to do so. The camp-tender was leaving for a new herder's camp. The cook had just fried a large batch of doughnuts and I hastily packed a few and sent them along.

The very next time the camp-tender went to that camp he returned with a present for me. It was a ten-pound bucket, filled to the brim with golden sugar-crusted doughnuts. I was touched, and showed them to the cook.

'These,' I remarked tactlessly, 'are the best-looking doughnuts I ever saw. Imagine a man making them!'

The cook did not share my enthusiasm. Her face went blank and her silence should have warned me.

'Let's have some for supper,' I said, getting out a plate.

'I baked cookies for supper,' she replied stiffly.

'Save them for tomorrow.' I was lifting the doughnuts out of the bucket now.

Her back went as rigid as a flagpole, and her lip poked out. I got the idea that she wasn't pleased but I didn't know just how to handle the situation without a loss of face. I left the kitchen hastily.

At supper we had both cookies and doughnuts. The men did not touch the cookies but they cleaned the plate of doughnuts. When the dishes were washed up, the cook folded her apron deliberately and asked for her time.

'I thought you liked it here,' I said reproachfully.

'No herder can insult me and get away with it,' she returned sullenly. 'If you folks like his cooking better than mine, give him my job.'

She had lived in the country longer than I and knew the herder's challenge for what it was. Nothing I could say would dissuade her. She left in a huff. A week passed before we found another cook, and long before that week was up I had lost my taste for doughnuts. But I still liked herders.

I had not lived here long enough to understand their peculiarities (and doubt that I ever will), but I had learned something that caused me to overlook even the loss of a cook. I had learned the meaning of the word *loyalty* in its truest sense. The word *shepherd* has always been a synonym for loyalty. I believe that this accounts for the fact that in no other business is a man of the herder's caliber entrusted with assets representing so great an amount of capital.

The herder is solely responsible for the welfare of approximately eighteen hundred head of sheep. An hour's neglect or carelessness on his part could turn the balance from profit to loss on the entire year's operation, and nobody knows it so well as he. There are few sacrifices the herder would not make to keep his flock intact.

In this country the herder is liable to a term in the penitentiary if he abandons his sheep in the mountains for any reason whatever; nor can he quit his job without first serving five days' notice to the woolgrower. The quality of a good herder's loyalty can be gauged by the fact that only once have I known one to abandon his sheep, and that man was crazy. Fear of the law does not influence them, because the penalty has been exercised so seldom that it has taken on the status of a myth. I doubt if half the herders in Montana even know of its existence. We have had herders who went to heartbreaking lengths to stay with their sheep, and one who laid down his life for them.

Years ago we had a herder whose name was Ed. He was one of the finest men I have ever known as well as the best herder we ever had. I can see him yet — on the crest of some wind-swept hill, with his dogs and sheep about him. A tall, gaunt man, with straight-seeing blue eyes and a ready smile.

His sheep were always fat and he prided himself on the fact that he could usually keep them that way on grass. They seldom required the cottonseed cake or corn that is often so necessary for the welfare of sheep in bitter winter weather. He used his head and planned each day's grazing as carefully as a pilot maps out his flight.

He knew every foot of the range and if there was grass to be had, Ed drove his sheep to it. No mountain was too high, no snow too deep. He never spared himself, and his pride in his flock was a splendid thing to see. He would trust them to no other herder and we could never persuade him to take so much as a few days' vacation. We were surprised and pleased, then, when one day the camp-tender brought word that Ed wanted a leave of absence.

We later discovered that he had spent all of two days' vacation in a Butte clinic and had been told by the doctors there that he had an incurable cancer of the stomach. He did not tell us, he never complained, and for a full year after the doctors had diagnosed his case, he stuck to his job.

At last the time came when the pain grew so intense that it was difficult for him to leave his wagon. He knew the end was near, and he worried for fear he might die on the range and leave his sheep unprotected. He selected a day when he was sure the camp-tender would bring supplies; bathed, shaved and dressed himself in his best suit of clothes. Then he lay down on his bunk, put his revolver to his head and shot himself. He had planned it all very carefully, at least two weeks in advance. The camp-tender told us later that he had noticed a penciled ring drawn about the date on Ed's calendar a fortnight before and had wondered about it.

Ed left a note for my husband. He explained the whole tragic situation and apologized for leaving his sheep alone even so short a time. He said he'd counted them an hour before and that they were all there. But should any be missing when the camp-tender came, he wanted pay for them deducted from his time.

To this day I can remember every word of that note. The last stark sentence still has the power to bring a lump to my throat:

Thank you for all your kindness to a fellow who did not know enough to appreciate it.

His poor tortured mind ... Counting all those years of loyalty as nothing against the fact that he felt he was betraying us in the end. . . .

His death saddened every man on the ranch, but you would never have known it. Death is a mystery that ranch men take in their stride. When I first came to Montana it seemed to me that they were casual and cold-blooded about it. I did not realize that there is no more sensitive or tender-hearted creature alive than the average ranch man or herder; that their casualness is merely a shell built up to conceal their real feelings.

I remember the weatherbeaten, hard-boiled chore boy (a man of fifty or thereabouts) who was given the unpleasant task of cleaning the wagon in which the suicide had taken place. The wagon had been pulled into the home ranch and I was forced to pass it on my way to the garden. The chore boy was scrubbing away. He had not heard me come and I was about to speak when I caught sight of his face. It was twisted with emotion and the tears were streaming down his leathery cheeks. I was humbled ... and ashamed for my intrusion. I would have slipped away quietly but he looked up and saw me. Instantly his expression changed to one of surliness.

'Looks like Ed'd ought to of remembered that some of us fellers 'ud have to clean up this mess,' he complained. 'Looks like he could've gone outside if he was hell-bent to splatter his brains around.'

We had another herder who shot himself accidentally while cleaning a gun. This herder could have reached the ranch in an hour had he deserted his herd to do so. Instead, he drove his flock in, over a period of four hours, and arrived at the ranch on the verge of collapse from loss of blood and exposure. We rushed him to the nearest hospital, and when he had had a blood transfusion Tom asked him how he had managed to travel that far in his weakened condition. The herder told him quite cheerfully that he had crawled the last half-mile. And he told the truth, for when the sheep were driven back over that same trail the next day, we found his loyalty patterned in a crimson ribbon on the snow.

As a rule the herder's sense of responsibility is confined to his own flock, but this is not always the case. Several winters ago two of our herders were camped within five miles of each other, with a mountain between. Once a week the camp-tender brought them supplies, and this was their only contact with the outside world. On a morning following the camp-tender's visit, a fierce blizzard swept the mountains. It raged for twenty-four hours, and shortly after it had died down one of the herders, a man whom we called Jean, picked up a hundred or more ewes whose brands he recognized as belonging to the flock of his neighbor.

He gave the matter little thought, but when toward nightfall another bunch wandered into his herd, he was puzzled and concerned. The next morning twenty more ewes sought sanctuary in his flock, and now Jean was convinced that all was not right in his neighbor's camp, else by this time the other herder would have corralled his band at the shearing pens (which was only three miles the other side of his camp) and he and his dogs would be scouring the country for lost sheep.

Jean did some tall thinking. He could not leave his own sheep to investigate, and yet if he failed to do so that other herd would be scattered beyond recall and perhaps half of them destroyed by coyotes before the camp-tender's next visit. Aside from that, he felt sure the other herder was ill or had met with some accident. He decided to go to his aid and he turned his flock toward his neighbor's camp.

The journey was fraught with hazards. The snow was deep and soft. His sheep floundered about in it and many times he was forced to dig some of them out of great drifts. It was dusk before he reached the other camp and he was tired to the point of collapse.

He was alarmed by what he saw. No ewes were on the bed-ground, and there was not a dog in sight. Nor had the sheep bedded there the night before; there were no tracks in the new snow about the wagon. But the thing that concerned him the most was the fact that no welcome curl of smoke rose skyward from the stovepipe. He tried the door and found that it had been locked from the inside. His fingers were stiff from cold, and none too steady. Ten minutes elapsed before he managed to break the lock.

Once Jean got inside, he could see the dim outline of the other herder's figure on the bunk. He was angry and disgusted. 'I figured I'd gone to all my trouble for a skunk who could hole in and sleep while his sheep ran loose,' he told us. 'I grabbed him by the shoulder and shook him ...'

He jumped back then and stared down in shocked dismay. The man on the bunk was dead; his body was stiff and cold. When he got hold of himself Jean covered him with a tarp. Then he kindled a fire in the stove and sat down to think.

At this point I wish I could say that he knew he had only to make himself comfortable and presently the dogs would return, driving the missing herd before them. I've read about such dogs, but ours are not of that breed. (Just once before I die I hope I can see or hear of a Montana sheep dog which has gathered up a flock of lost sheep and brought them in alone.)

It didn't take Jean long to piece the story out. A high wind had been blowing for three days. Sheep have a habit of traveling in the direction of the wind. In the absence of the herder they had set out and the dogs, lacking their usual instructions, had followed. They would continue to follow, striving to keep the flock together. Their efforts would be futile, but they would stick with the herd until their feet gave out and then they would return to camp, alone.

For Jean to corral his own sheep at the shearing pen and set out for help would mean the loss of a day, in which time the lost sheep would be scattered all over the county. He did not relish the idea of spending several nights alone with a dead man, but he stayed just the same. The next morning he corralled his sheep and set out in the direction of the wind. Eventually he picked up most of the sheep and the dogs, and drove both herds into the ranch.

Surprisingly, he was little the worse for his experience, which he related in minute detail. I could scarcely wait for him to be through because, woman-like, I was curious to know where he had slept all those nights. I finally asked him. For the first time he displayed a touch of resentment. His face became crimson with embarrassment. 'Where could I sleep?' he demanded heatedly. 'There ain't but one bunk. I had to sleep if I hunted those sheep, so I just shoved Bill over and slept long side of him.'

I stared at the man for a moment and then left the room abruptly. When I later voiced my horror, Tom reminded me of something I had forgotten. Jean had risked his life, and the welfare of his own flock, to go to the aid of his fellow herder. And it was Jean who later 'shot his stake' to place a fitting marker on his grave.

If men are rewarded in the Hereafter for what they endure on earth, the herder has something to look forward to. I think I can say, with no fear of contradiction, that sheepherding is the hardest, most harrowing job on earth. Ditch-digging is child's play beside it. In all other professions there is a limit to the number of hours a man may work. The shepherd's job is a twenty-four-hour job. He can never be sure when he collapses in his bunk at night that he will be able to stay there until morning. It is second nature for him to sleep with one ear on his sheep and the other on his dogs.

If the dog gives warning that a coyote is stalking the flock, the herder jerks out of a sodden sleep, grabs his gun and fires a shot which he hopes will frighten the marauder away. It seldom does. Sometimes he is forced to repeat the procedure four or five times before morning.

One of the most aggravating habits sheep have is that of wandering off the bed-ground at night. In winter a high wind is almost sure to precipitate an epidemic of wanderlust. In summer, the mosquitoes will have the same effect. Sometimes a lead sheep will decide that she has not had her fill of green grass and set out to remedy the lack; whereupon every sheep in the herd will do likewise. Sometimes they just leave — for no good reason at all. It may be simply an idea that can be promptly squelched, or it may become an obsession. If the latter, there will be little sleep for the herder.

But his nocturnal problems sink into insignificance before the problems of his days — especially in winter. Our winters are always cold, but several years ago we had an unusually bitter winter. The wind blew for days on end with no letup and the thermometer dropped down to thirty below and stayed there. Thirty below is not bad in this country if it's calm, but a high wind can drive it into the marrow of your bones. It can also drive it through any sheep wagon that has ever been built.

We had a good thirty days of this before we got any reaction from the herders, and then one morning the camptender brought word that a herder wanted to quit. He was brought by the ranch to get his time and Tom asked him what his grievance was. He refused to say at first, but when Tom insisted he sullenly replied that he didn't see why he had to have the coldest camp on the range.

'Nonsense,' Tom told him. 'Your camp isn't any colder than Joe's [a herder with a camp some four miles away], and he isn't quitting.'

'It is colder too,' the disgruntled one replied. 'Joe's only slept with his spuds four nights this winter and I've had to sleep with mine every night for a month.'

And sleeping with potatoes to keep them from freezing represents a very small share of a herder's trials. If a sheep gets her fill in the winter she must forage from sunup until dusk. If she fails to get a 'fill' every day, she grows gaunt and has to be trucked to the home ranch and thrown into the hospital band. The hospital band is composed of weak sheep, which could not weather the winter without corn or cottonseed cake. At best there are always a few sheep which normally swell this band — very old sheep or lame sheep. A herder's efficiency is judged in relative proportion to the number of sheep he turns into the hospital band in a winter.

If he values his reputation or even his job, the herder must drive his sheep off the bed-ground at sunup, blizzard or no. Before he leaves camp his potatoes and canned goods must be wrapped securely in his roll of bedding, to prevent freezing.

His lunch consists of one sandwich, which he tucks in the pocket of his sheepskin. At night he returns to his wagon, having trudged many miles in the wake of his sheep, to find his fire in ashes and his water bucket frozen hard. He builds his fire, thaws out his water bucket and cooks a sketchy meal for his dogs and himself. His menu seldom varies. Day after day his food is fried food, since he has neither time nor energy to prepare any other.

Good weather or bad, herders have their troubles. I spent most of my first winter in Montana feeling sorry for them. Every time a blizzard whistled through the sturdy windows of our house, I remembered the herder's flimsy shelters, and when the blizzard broke and the sun came out, I was always relieved. I didn't know then that the blinding reflection of the sun on the snow could cause the herder pain, or at best discomfort.

The sun's rays can penetrate the best of smoked glasses and cause the eyes to throb and sting. Loss or accident to his glasses renders the herder helpless and often results in the tragedy of snow-blindness. The native herder would never dream of starting to work without his colored glasses, but it is hard to convince a herder who comes up from the Southern States that these are a necessity. They usually buy a pair or two when they first arrive, as a sort of keeping-up-with-the-Joneses gesture, but they are constantly breaking them or forgetting to take them along.

Tom seldom employs out-of-state herders, but there are times when herders are scarce and he is forced to hire anyone he can get. This was true immediately after the First World War. During that time, he employed a herder from Arizona. One morning in February the man was digging into the pocket of his sheepskin coat for a sack of tobacco. His colored glasses were caught in the drawstring, and they fell against a rock and were broken into bits.

It was cloudy that morning and he suffered no discomfort for a time. Later the sun came out and reflected on the snow, but the herder was a long way from his camp and second pair of glasses, and he was not as energetic as he might have been. Some people's eyes are more sensitive to snow glare than others, and the herder proved to be one of these people.

He did not recognize the danger signals as a native herder would have done. His eyes began to smart, but he was in acute pain before he realized the seriousness of the situation. He sent the dogs around the sheep, turned them and started back for his camp. He had covered only about half the distance when he lost his vision. Panic took him. He did not stop to think or reason; he had but one plan and that was to reach his wagon as soon as possible, and he stumbled along in that general direction as fast as he dared.

There was an abandoned prospect hole directly in his path and he walked right into it, striking his head a nasty lick on supporting timbers as he fell. He also fractured an ankle and his collarbone. He would surely have died from exposure if a Ranger had not been searching for a strayed horse that day.

The Ranger spotted the sheep from a hill and rode down to them, hoping their herder had seen his horse. By then the sheep were a good half-mile from the prospect hole. The

Ranger was puzzled when he failed to find the herder and thoughtful enough to ride by the ranch and report the matter to Tom.

Herders who are new to this section have such a capacity for getting into trouble that Tom was alarmed and sent three riders out to search. The snow was fresh and it did not take them long to track him. The man was unconscious and could be no help to them. One of the riders was lowered into the hole with a rope which he tied about the injured herder, and the rescue was accomplished. Months passed before the Arizonan could get about again, but the moment he was able to discard his crutches, he took a south-bound train.

Out-of-state herders do not have a corner on this capacity for trouble. Strange things can happen to veteran native herders, through no act of carelessness on their part. One of our friends had a herder who went through a harrowing experience a few springs past. The day was warm and sunny and the herder was tired. He was also sleepy. Coyotes had scattered his flock the night before, and he had spent a good many hours rounding them up and driving them back to the bed-ground. The sheep were now grazing contentedly in an area where the grass was thick, so the herder sat down with his back against a big rock and promptly dozed off. One of his arms rested along the top of the boulder.

He was awakened by a stab of pain in his finger and he leaped to his feet in time to see a huge rattler slithering along the ground a short distance away. The herder was petrified with fear. He had a fever sore on his lip and he knew that should he attempt to suck the poison from the wound, this would be suicide.

There was no time to think. His hand was beginning to swell and two angry pin points of red were plainly discernible on the tip of one of his fingers. Before he could possibly reach help, he would die, and the thought of dying a tortured death, alone in the mountains, was more than he could contemplate.

There was but one thing to do and this he did quickly. He always carried a big knife which he used to pelt his dead sheep. He got the knife out of his pocket and performed a neat job of surgery on the injured finger, cutting it off to the first joint. Then he sped back to his wagon and stopped the bleeding with soot from the inside of the stovelid.

The Lord had his arms around that herder. By every law of science and medicine, an infection should certainly have resulted. Six hours elapsed before he received a doctor's care, and yet the finger healed perfectly.

10

And not so good

Tom accuses me of persistently ignoring the fact that all herders are not good herders. One day last summer he came into the living-room and caught me entertaining an Eastern dude with one of my favorite stories of a certain herder's loyalty. The moment she got into her car and drove away he said: 'You have the darndest way of never seeing anything you don't want to see. Why didn't you tell her about some of the worthless herders we've had?'

'She wouldn't be interested.'

'Well, I am — and you ought to be. Half the problems of the sheep business today come from an increasing lack of good herders, and you know it.'

Thereupon he proceeded to recall to my memory herders of ours who had allowed their sheep to overgraze the range through ignorance or laziness, whose indifference and carelessness had resulted in every calamity to which sheep are prone.

I argued that most of the men he had mentioned were not herders in the truest sense of the word; a number of them were 'drifters' who did not even own a bed-roll — the 'guinea stamp' of the true herder. They had not taken up herding as a profession because the life appealed to them, but for various other reasons. Some were crazy, some were hiding from the law, and a good half-dozen had been habitual drinkers who had taken to the mountains only because they could not hold down a job in town where liquor was plentiful. When Tom quite suddenly lost all interest in the subject, I was sure he agreed with me.

I had heard the expression 'as crazy as a herder' all my life, but I lived in Montana two years before I met my first crazy herder. I was completely happy that summer. At last I had a job which was as interesting as it was useful, and I had begun to feel at home.

I acquired the job after a painful process of elimination in which it was finally decided that my usefulness began and ended behind the steering-wheel of a car or truck. Back in Texas I had been considered a good driver. I even knew a little about the mechanics of an engine, and could take care of the simpler things that went wrong, like cleaning spark plugs and blowing out a clogged gas line.

As soon as I overcame my first fear of mountain driving, there was no road too steep for me to tackle, no trail too rough. This really surprised me no end. I was still afraid to walk or ride horseback alone. The howl of a coyote could strike terror in my heart, and even the sight of a porcupine, the most harmless of all wild life in Montana and the most common, did queer things to my spine. But once I got behind the familiar wheel of a car, fear promptly left me.

They needed a driver badly at the ranch — to run errands, carry messages to Cherry Creek and Sunrise, and generally pinch-hit for the Boss and the camp-tender. It gave me enormous satisfaction to know that I saved them many hours on the road which they could use to good advantage for more important tasks. Sometimes, when the herders' wagons were not far from the house I'd even deliver their mail or take up things that could not wait for the camp-tender's regular weekly visit. It was on one such errand that I came in contact with a crazy herder. The camp-tender had been up to this man's wagon that morning and forgot to take some 'snoose' (snuff).

Everyone on a sheep ranch understands that a herder out of 'snoose' is a wrathful and put-upon herder, especially if the 'snoose' had been marked down on his current order. Somebody had to go to his camp again that day and I offered to do it. I got a roll (six cans) of Copenhagen from the cellar commissary and, accompanied by my twelve-year-old sister, who was visiting me, set out.

We ran onto the man and his flock before we reached his wagon. My sister wanted to gather some wild flowers, and I sat down on the running-board of the car and visited with the herder while she did so.

He was very reserved and awfully shy. I tried my best to put him at ease, with little success. The more I talked, the more silent he became. I was casting about in my mind for something to say when an inquisitive old ewe walked up and began to eye us fixedly. She had the slyest eyes I had ever seen and presently I said to the herder, 'That ewe looks exactly like a malicious old woman gossip.'

In a flash the herder's shyness vanished. He leaped to his feet and towered above me, his face wreathed in smiles. 'You think so too, Missus?' he whispered hoarsely. 'You think sheep look like people? I'll tell you a secret if you don't tell the Boss. *They are people!* Same as you and me. Look at that one,' he gestured violently. 'She's a nice little girl. She's pretty and cute. And that one's old and ugly — and that one's young and mean; she'll walk right over the rest to get what she wants...'

I dragged my horrified eyes from one sheep to another. A cold shiver ran up and down my spine as it suddenly dawned on me that the man was insane. The worst of it was that I thought I must be crazy too. He told the truth, those sheep *did* look like people... The longer I looked, the more I knew that this was a good place not to be, but I couldn't move. I might have been glued to that running-board.

A dog ran up and leaped upon his master, and miraculously the man quit gesturing and lapsed into gloomy silence. I called my sister and got away quickly, but it was months before I could bear to look a sheep in the face and when I eventually forced myself to it, it was an exquisite relief to find they looked like sheep again.

This is the Land of Promise for the man who is hiding from the law. Not because the natives of this country would knowingly abet a lawbreaker. The natives have a wholesome respect for the law, but they also have a deep-rooted quirk of character which at times defeats the very thing it would respect and uphold. They accept strangers at face value. Until a man is proven otherwise he is presumed to be everything he has claimed. In all these years I have never known Tom to ask a stranger for a recommendation or question him in any way, and strange as it may seem, his trust is often justified.

I have said before that many of our habits and customs are influenced and colored by the habits and customs of pioneer days, and I've often wondered if this lack of curiosity on the native's part is not a throwback to a day when it wasn't healthy or profitable to probe into another man's past — when guns answered questions and dead men told no tales.

At any rate I've always contended that a little adroit questioning at the start might have resulted in our not hiring a number of herders and ranch men who were later discovered to be hiding from the law. We've employed, unknowingly, horse and cattle thieves, stickup men, bigamists, army deserters, alimony-dodgers and once even a man who was later convicted of murder.

The murderer, I'm sure, was crazy. To this good day it is hard for me to believe that gentle old John could have killed a flea. He was a splendid herder, conscientious in his care of the sheep, kind and understanding with his dogs.

I have seen this man, who was twice convicted of murder after he left our employ, agonize over a dog which had tangled with a porcupine. He worked for hours on end, with infinite patience and tenderness, in an effort to extract quills from the animal's muzzle, chest and paws. And when the quills broke off or were too short to be reached with pliers, he did what few men would have done: he extracted those quills with his teeth.

Yet old John committed murder. He killed a miner in the heat of passion and was convicted. Good behavior over a number of years won him a parole. He had not been free a week before he got into an argument with another man over a card game and killed again. This time there were several witnesses and he was sent up for life.

Once the sheriff came to Stonyacres when haying was almost over and arrested our stacker for stealing a saddle horse. We were dismayed. There was not another stacker in the crew; if the sheriff took his prisoner away that day it would hold up haying for the length of time it took to replace him. And this was to have been our last day of haying.

I still smile whenever I think of the conversation that took place between Tom and the sheriff.

'Look here,' Tom said, 'we're almost through haying and it looks like snow. If you take George now we may catch a storm tomorrow and be held up for a month. Why can't you go on back home and let me bring him over tonight?'

The sheriff shook his head regretfully. 'I can't do that,' he said. 'But I'll tell you what I will do: I'll pitch in and help and we'll finish this job in time for me to get the prisoner to jail before dark.' Whereupon he rolled up his sleeves, grabbed a pitchfork and began to clean up the loose hay around the stack.

We had another hay-digger who was a stickup man, hiding from the law the year he worked for us. He had successfully put over a clever holdup on a near-by small-town bank. He walked boldly into an automobile salesroom in a city a hundred miles from his contemplated robbery and announced that he wished to purchase a car immediately. He claimed that he had that day completely wrecked his own car and suffered numerous head and face injuries in the wreck. His face was swathed in bandages and he reeked of antiseptics, so it never occurred to the delighted salesman to doubt his word.

It was arranged that the salesman should take him on a trial drive. No sooner had the two reached the outskirts of the city than the stickup man poked a gun in the salesman's

ribs and warned him to do his bidding or take the consequences. The salesman had no alternative, and he drove
the car in the direction named.

The stickup man was a chatty fellow. He confided his
contemplated holdup to the now terrified salesman in intricate detail. He boasted of his cleverness. And strangely
enough, he took a liking to his chauffeur. When they presently reached a lonely stretch of road, some ten miles from
their destination, he told the salesman to stop the car and
get out. But first he named a lonely place not too far distant, where he amicably agreed to leave the car as soon as
his mission was accomplished.

The bandit was familiar with the routine of the bank he
planned to rob, because he chose the lunch hour for his
holdup. The cashier was alone at the time and the bandit
walked boldly into the bank, pulled a gun on the man and
forced him to hand over several thousand dollars in cur-
rency. Then he made a neat getaway and drove the car
swiftly to the place agreed upon, when he took the bandages
off his face and disappeared.

The mystery of that holdup was not solved for more than
two years, and it would never have been solved had not the
bandit made the mistake that wiser men than he have made.
He boasted of his cleverness to a woman who later betrayed
him to the law.

One of the bigamists who worked for us was an easy-
going, good-natured fellow, but not much of a herder. He
disliked trouble and ill feeling and he neglected to confide to
a current bride her exact *status quo*. He was careless of his
letters and papers and the woman in looking them over discovered that he had failed to get a divorce from her prede-
cessor. She accused him and he walked out on her. She was
smart, and she tracked him all the way from Oregon and informed the law of his whereabouts.

The sheriff telephoned Tom that he had a warrant for the man's arrest. Tom sent another herder up to take his place, and when the sheriff brought his charge by the ranch to settle up before returning to the county seat, Tom asked, 'What seems to be the trouble?'

Before the sheriff could reply the herder reddened and grinned. 'They tell me I have too many wives,' he announced.

Tom was surprised. 'That's news to me. I didn't even know you were married.'

'Hell, yes!' the herder boasted. 'I've had five wives in my time. I might as well tell you because it'll all come out now. But I shore hate to think about going to jail.'

'Man alive!' Tom exclaimed. 'You're in luck. If you really have five wives, jail's the safest place you can be.'

We had another bigamist herder who was a surly fellow with an ungovernable temper. He became angry with a dog and booted him to death. He was still kicking the dog's limp dead body in a frenzy of rage when a lamber arrived on the scene. Horrified, the lamber tried to pull him away and the herder picked up a stone and let him have it in the head. The lamber was knocked out, but when he came to he walked down to the ranch and reported the matter. Tom swore out a charge of assault and had the herder arrested. The sheriff informed us several days later that the man was wanted for bigamy in another state.

I remember one of our herders who had been dodging alimony payments for twenty years. He was a frugal man and seldom drew more than a few dollars at a time over a period of several years. This is a practice which does not appeal to Tom because, inevitably, the herder will choose a time to quit or draw his accumulated wages when our bank account is at its lowest ebb.

When this man had around two thousand dollars due him Tom wrote out a check for that amount and insisted that he take it. The herder refused the check. He said: 'I don't want it now. You just keep it until I take a lay-off. Then I'll get the money and put it in my cache.'

'Good God, man,' Tom exclaimed, 'don't tell me you're burying your money!'

Grudgingly the herder admitted that he was, but he assured Tom that the cache was perfectly safe.

'Nothing's perfectly safe except the vaults of a bank,' Tom warned him, 'and that's where you'd better put it.'

The herder was obstinate. They argued for some time and finally the man broke down and confessed that he dared not bank his money, that he owed his ex-wife twenty years' accumulated alimony. She was still alive; he was afraid she'd get wind of a bank account and try to attach it.

'I'm not onery,' he tried to explain, 'or stingy either. If she'd married a decent hard-working fellow I'd of kept on paying her alimony. But she didn't. She married a lazy, worthless skunk, that never did a day's work in his life. Soon as I heard about it I made up my mind I wasn't going to support him. I quit a good job and lit out.'

Tom had a hard time convincing him that the need to pay alimony ceased to exist when his wife had remarried. He was a blissful herder when he finally got that through his head. The first thing he said was 'Oh boy! Now I can use my own name again.'

The herder who drinks is usually a pretty good herder when he's on the job, but he's undependable. When the craving for drink hits him he insists upon going to town, however inconvenient the time may be. He will hatch up every conceivable excuse to gain his end and none will be the real one. The woolgrower is good at sidetracking these

phony excuses, but occasionally he will drive a herder too
far and the man will quit his job. To save his face, he will
have to think up some grievance which will justify asking
for his 'time,' but he's an adept at this. If he happens not
to be in an inventive frame of mind he can always resort to
an old-time trick. He can order delicacies which he is sure
will not be brought to him, and when they fail to appear, he
can give notice without loss of face.

Not so long ago one of our herders decided suddenly that
he must have a lay-off. Men were scarce this year and Tom
sought to dissuade him. He wore down every excuse the
herder had to offer and came home confident that he had
postponed an untimely drunk.

The camp-tender came in from the man's camp a few
days later and said, 'Dan wants to quit.'

Tom looked crestfallen. 'I thought I had him talked out
of going to town. He seemed all right when I left his camp.'

The camp-tender grinned and held out a slip of paper.
'He's not all right now. He's ordered canned oysters, fresh
pineapple and mushrooms.' That was enough. Tom telephoned the employment agency in Butte to start looking for
another herder.

Drinking herders are, beyond doubt, the most improvi-
dent class of men I have ever known. As a rule, so long as
they stay in camp, they're extremely frugal. They seldom
spend a cent except for clothing, tobacco and perhaps a
subscription to their home-town paper or favorite pulp
magazine. But once they get into town they spend with the
passionate abandon of a sailor who has not made port in
several years. We have had herders who have 'shot their
stakes' of several hundred dollars in a few days and returned to the ranch broke, discouraged and deeply in debt.

The drinking herder goes into town with his eyes open.

He knows he is going to spend every penny he possesses, along with as much of his next year's wages as his credit is good for. The dentist in the small town which is fifteen miles from our ranch told me a story that illustrates this state of affairs perfectly.

He had a patient who was a drinking herder. Every time this man got into town he made a bee-line for the dentist's office and handed him over the price of a new set of 'store teeth.' He had no illusions about himself, he knew he would either lose or break his plates when once he got 'going good' on a spree. The dentist is a kindly, unselfish man and after he had made four sets of plates for his patient, he tried to remonstrate with the man.

'See here,' he said, 'why don't you just leave your teeth with me until you're sober? You'd save a lot of money.'

'Nope,' the herder replied firmly. 'I'd spend the money anyway and I need my teeth to eat with until I'm clean laid out. I gotta have them.'

And so for a number of years, until, in fact, the herder left our Valley, the dentist could absolutely depend upon making at least one set of teeth for his patient each year.

One excuse that the drinking herder works overtime is an aching tooth. Now, the woolgrower has no defense against an aching tooth, the herder knows it. In his heart the woolgrower may feel that the aching tooth is nothing more than a figment of the herder's imagination, but he dares not take a chance. A herder who is actually in pain can't herd sheep properly.

One summer, when our sheep were on the Forest, two herders developed toothache in the course of one month. They both went to town, stayed there drunk for a week, and when later Tom checked with the dentist, neither had been near his office.

Tom had wasted a lot of time getting them back and forth, and he was furious. It takes several hours to reach our allotment in the Forest. The road is steep and narrow, with numerous hairpin curves. It is only in the past few years that it has been made safe for motor travel, and I would say it is none too safe now. At any rate it is not a road one would travel for pleasure, although the scenery is spectacular and breath-takingly beautiful — if one dared raise one's eyes from the road to take it in.

So when a third herder rode horseback to the Ranger Station and telephoned that he must get down to the dentist, Tom's patience was exhausted. He got in touch with the dentist, who agreed to go up to the Forest and extract the fellow's tooth. When they eventually found him he was overjoyed to see Tom and a man whom he supposed to be a substitute herder. His face fell ludicrously when he recognized the dentist.

'I can't spare you, Bill,' Tom informed him, 'so I brought the dentist up to pull your tooth.' The herder looked panic-stricken for a moment but he was a good sport. He sat against a boulder and let the dentist extract his tooth.

When the dentist got back to the ranch he told me that he had almost balked when the herder indicated what he suspected was, and later found to be, a perfectly sound tooth. The dentist had lived in this country long enough to know that the herder would have sacrificed every tooth in his head rather than have his bluff called. He would have been outraged and resentful had his deception been exposed.

The summer following this episode Tom decided to nip the toothache excuse in the bud. The first time a herder sent word that he had to go to the dentist, Tom again asked the dentist to go up to the Forest. To their surprise and concern they found the patient half crazy with pain. His face was horribly swollen and he was running a temperature from a badly infected gum. Several days before he had attempted to pry out the tooth with the sharp end of a file, had broken it off at the roots and lacerated his gum. The dentist bundled the man into the car and started for a hospital, leaving Tom to herd his sheep until a man could be brought to relieve him.

I recall one drinking herder who wrung my heart for a number of years. Tom declared that my sympathy would not have been so long-lived had the fellow hailed from any state but Texas.

He came from a small inland town which was quite near the city where I was raised. The man was both a herder and shearer and he had wandered into Montana with a crew of Mexican shearers who worked for us that year. When the shearing season was over he got on a big drunk. The crew went on to their next job, leaving him penniless and stranded in a strange country. He had heard that I was a Texan and he waylaid me in town one day and begged me to find him a job. He was a smooth talker and enlisted my sympathy at once. I persuaded Tom, against his better judgment, to take him on, and I knew his life history before he had been on the ranch an hour.

He hated Montana. He hated the cold and the mountains, and his one urge in life was to accumulate enough money to get back to Texas. He had a feeble old mother there, and he was fearful lest she die before he could see her again.

He herded for a full year, got a stake and bade us a joyous farewell. He was going home. I rejoiced with him. But he never got home. He met up with some friends in Butte, got crazy drunk and lost his stake.

He was very humble when he crept back to the ranch. He wept bitter tears when he related his experiences to me.

He berated himself for the lack of will power that might well be the cause of his never seeing his sweet old mother again.

So moved was I that I pleaded with Tom to take a chance and lend him the price of a ticket to Texas, and I must confess that I thought Tom was heartless when he flatly refused. 'I'm not contributing a dime to the upkeep of the Butte saloons,' he said. 'That is what it would amount to. If he really has a *sweet old mother* and wants to see her again, someone is going to have to knock him in the head, buy his ticket and dump him on a south-bound train. He'll never get any farther than Butte by himself.'

How true his predictions were! A year later the Texan again bade us a jubilant farewell. He declared his intention of going straight to the depot the moment he got to Butte and never budging from the place until his train pulled out. He was back at the ranch in ten days with the same old story. I suffered with him this time too, but I did not suffer to the extent that I was willing to lend him the price of a railway ticket. The next year the same procedure had to be gone through.

Each time the herder's remorse was pitiful to see. All he could talk about was his old mother and the Lone Star State. When we had lived through four of these experiences, Tom lost patience.

'Look here,' he said to the herder on the occasion of his last return, 'do you really want to go back to Texas?' Oh, yes, yes, the herder did, more than anything else in the world.

'All right, then, promise me you'll do exactly as I say when you get another stake, and I'll see that you get to Texas.'

The herder promised eagerly and when he got another stake together Tom accompanied him to Butte. He refused to give him a penny and he rode herd on him until train time. He sat in the barber shop while the herder bathed and got shaved, he went to a store with him and helped him pick out some 'boughten' clothes, which he paid for. He took him to the bank and had all his money not needed for direct expense of the trip changed into one travelers' check. The herder signed the check as he was told, without in the least knowing what it was all about. Tom did not enlighten him then.

As they came out of the bank they ran onto some of the herder's friends, who greeted him enthusiastically and insisted that he come and have a farewell drink. Tom refused for him. By now the Texan was beginning to weaken. He was dry. He looked over his shoulder longingly at his retreating friends, and caught Tom by the arm.

'Look, Boss,' he pleaded, 'just give me five dollars so's I can treat the boys before I go. I won't touch a drop. I swear I won't.'

'No,' Tom replied firmly, 'you save that five dollars to treat the Texas boys with when you get back home.'

Eventually train time rolled around and they went to the depot. When the ticket was bought, Tom took the herder into the dining car and gave the steward fifteen dollars. 'See that you don't eat any more than that,' he warned the herder, 'or you'll have to go hungry until you get to Dallas.'

Three minutes before the train was scheduled to leave, Tom took the travelers' check out of his pocket. 'Do you know what this is?' he asked. The herder didn't, but he was curious to know what he had signed.

'It's a travelers' check,' Tom told him. '*A travelers' check*. See? You can't cash it until you get to Dallas and you'll be arrested if you try!'

So, at long last, the Texan went home.

11

The sheep dog

OUR trucks are on the road constantly now, hauling the rams back and forth from the various bands of ewes; supplying the camps with wood, salt and cottonseed cake. Winter has really come, and there will be no letup until the chinook winds transform the snow into miniature rivulets and lakes.

The snow on the grade that leads out is hard and packed and, from the upper panes of my study windows, ruts made by the trucks look like giant furrows. I cannot see out of the lower panes, for they are crusted with etchings of ice. Incongruously, these etchings resemble the waving ferns and palms of the tropics.

The air has been still and bitterly cold for a week and a filmy mist hangs over Wigwam Creek. Sounds carry with astonishing clarity but they are winter sounds now — the brittle crackle of the branches of the cottonwoods, the crunch of an overshoe, the shifting of snow on the roof — sounds I have learned to love....

Yesterday, as I feverishly addressed belated Christmas cards (for Christmas will soon be here) I heard a sound that is all too familiar in Montana — the clink-clink-clink of a broken cross-chain on car or truck. A few moments later one of our big trucks came rattling down the hill. As usual there followed a chorus of welcoming barks from the several old sheep dogs retired on the place. Familiar sounds ... And then the sudden squeal of brakes and the agonized howl of a dog ...

I tore down the steps and ... *I saw a dog die.* A faithful brown-and-white friend, whose failing eyesight and awkward body had betrayed him. I pushed the men aside, dropped down to the hard-packed snow and took his shaggy head on my lap. He looked up at me with fast glazing eyes ... a shudder passed over his body and then it went limp ...

I did not wait to see them take him away — or look back as I walked blindly toward the house. I knew that gentle hands would do all left to be done. And now a scarlet splotch on snow and a stark little mound of frozen earth bear witness that Buster is gone. But I do not need these mute reminders of a dog grown clumsy and tired and old from years of faithful service. For a long, long time a friendly, welcoming bark will strike a chord of sadness in my heart ...

A herder's best friend is his dog, and this loyal companion puts in as many hours and covers twenty times as much territory each day as the herder himself. The sheep dog possesses an uncanny intuition. He can sense restlessness in the herd much sooner than the herder. The very moment a lead sheep decides she'd prefer the grass on a distant hillside to that all about her, the dog is on his feet, quivering with excitement, and ready to drive her back.

Two things are instilled into the sheep dog from puppyhood: obedience to the herder and loyalty to the herd. It takes infinite patience and skill to train a sheep dog. Puppies are taken from their mothers at an early age on our ranch. They are isolated from every member of the outfit save the man who feeds them. All overtures of affection on their part are repulsed, lest they become attached to their caretaker and return to the ranch after they have been put to work.

They are not even permitted the company of the older dogs for fear they may acquire two bad habits that would render them worthless as sheep dogs — barking and chasing rabbits. A good sheep dog barks only when it is necessary to turn or discipline the sheep. To a sheep, a bark means business and too much of it means exactly nothing at all. A mature dog may chase rabbits in his leisure hours, but never when he's working. If a pup has acquired this habit before he's put to work, it's quite a job to cure him.

When obedience has become second nature, the pup is taken to a sheep camp, where the larger part of his training comes from a seasoned sheep dog. He learns readily, because sheep are in his blood; for generations his sires have followed the flocks to stand or fall in their protection. At first the young dog merely imitates the older one, but later he develops a technique of his own. When he has perfected this technique, he is a seasoned sheep dog.

A herder works his dogs almost entirely by signals because his voice could not be heard at any distance. The dogs race to the lead of the sheep, stop and look back to their master for instructions. An upraised arm to the right or left designates the direction the herd is to be turned.

Isolated as the herder is from the outside world, I believe the dog's companionship and devotion means as much as his work. Herders are ordinarily an easy-going lot, but a real or fancied abuse of their dogs can change them into surly avengers.

I recall one herder whose dog, old Floss, periodically roamed the hills at night after the sheep were bedded down. No effort on the part of the herder could break her of this habit. She was always on hand for work in the morning, however, and the herder was so fond of her that he eventually overlooked her wanderlust and ceased to concern himself about it.

One morning Floss failed to return. The herder searched for hours and finally found her caught in a trap and nearly dead. Government trappers put out these traps each winter and they are of incalculable value to the sheepman in his war against coyotes. Herders are always notified when traps are set out in their grazing area, and this herder had been notified.

It was a long way back to camp but the man carried the dog in his arms. She lived two days, and Tom happened by as she was breathing her last. Had chance not sent him by there would have been one less trapper on the Government payroll. The herder had worked himself into a blind rage. Tom could not make him see reason. He was going to finish the *so-and-so* who was responsible for Floss's death. He flourished his rifle violently and in the end it had to be taken from him by force. It was months before Floss's master could be convinced that the fault was his own for not tying her up at night, and when he eventually became convinced, his remorse was pitiful to see.

We seldom raise a 'one-man' dog. As a rule the sheep dog will work faithfully for any herder who is kind to him. Occasionally, however, we do have a dog which will not work for another herder when his first master has been taken away.

Mike, dog of the herder Ed, who killed himself, was one of these. He refused to work, although he had been one of the best dogs in the outfit. Again and again he was taken to a sheep camp, but he always turned up at the home ranch within a few hours. The last trail his master took, so far as he knew, ended here. His grief twisted our hearts. He would take food from none of us, and when hunger drove him he would come at night to the kitchen door and eat from a pan of food that was always left there.

At first we tried to make friends with him, but he distrusted us all. I think he felt we were in some way responsible for the loss of his master. We were forced to retire him when he was only four years old, although the average sheep dog works until he is ten at least. As the years went by he became rheumatic, blind, deaf and toothless, but he never forgot... Always there was that heart-breaking tenseness of waiting about him — that still patient listening for footsteps he knew and adored.

Mike disappeared about two years ago. We hunted for days, fearful lest he had got caught in a coyote trap or met with some other accident. We never found him and were forced to conclude that he had crawled off to some isolated spot to die alone. We never found his body, but not long ago a strange thing happened. A trapper rode through the ranch and stopped for lunch. At the table he asked Tom if he had lost a dog recently. He had seen the carcass of a dog near the camp where Mike's master had put an end to his life.

Tom replied that all of our dogs were accounted for and the conversation swung into another channel. After the trapper had ridden away I said to Tom, 'That dog could have been Mike.'

'I've been wondering just how long it would take you to fit Mike into the trapper's story,' he announced. 'Well, it couldn't have been Mike because that camp is a good fifteen miles from here. The poor old beggar could never have reached it, no matter how hard he tried.'

But I want to believe it. I want to believe that he tried with the last ounce of strength left in his poor wasted body to reach the spot where he had last worked sheep with his master.

There is a story of one dog's loyalty and heroism that stands out from all the rest in my mind, perhaps because it took place when I first came to Montana. I have never told this story but once. I told it at a dinner party when I was visiting in Texas and not one person at that dinner believed me. I have never since had the courage to face the incredulous expressions of my friends. I cannot prove this story. I have only the herder Sandy's word for it, but Sandy's word was his bond, and Sandy had a huge she-bear's pelt to substantiate his story.

The story concerns a pup of the old dog Floss, who later met her death in a trap. Her puppies were almost a month old when Tom and I returned from our honeymoon. We went down to the sheep shed and stood beside an enclosing panel watching five nondescript little bundles of fat and fur tumble about in the straw.

'Aren't they beauties?' Tom exclaimed enthusiastically.

I didn't think they were beauties. My conception of a sheep dog had been derived from the movies, and certainly these fat, multi-colored creatures did not measure up to that standard.

Tom called to the camp-tender, who was busy in another part of the shed, 'I thought you said there were six.'

'That's right.' The camp-tender pointed out one fat little fellow, curled up in a patch of sunlight, away from the rest. 'And he's the pick of the litter.'

'Derned if he doesn't look like a collie,' Tom said.

He did look different from the rest. For one thing he was larger and there was delicate symmetry in the set of his slender head, in the contours of his small round body. Nor was his coat drab and unpredictable in color. It held tawny lights that gave promise of a future magnificent bronze.

'He acts like a collie. Watch him.' The camp-tender whistled softly. The puppy's ears jerked alert and he scrambled up on small unsteady legs and raced toward us, his tail wagging furiously. I knelt down and put my hand through the panel and an ecstatic pink tongue shot out and began to lick my fingers.

I looked at his mother, puzzled. She was a small black bitch with a short, round muzzle and floppy ears. 'It's hard to believe this pup belongs to her,' I said. 'Just what breed of dogs are they, anyway?'

Tom grinned. 'Collie, shepherd and just plain cur.' I scratched the pup's silky head while he explained that a collie's feet will not stand up in rough, mountainous country; that a shepherd, though tough-footed, lacks the collie's superior strength; that the common cur supplies the all-needful endurance, and that the cross of these three breeds makes a perfect sheep dog.

'What's his name?' I wanted to know.

'He hasn't one yet. Some herder will name him.'

'Let me name him,' I begged. 'Let's call him Bogus because he looks like a collie — and isn't.'

At six months Bogus was taller than his mother. His small round body had thinned out to a wiry gracefulness. He had all the earmarks of a fine sheep dog, with one exception. He was far too friendly. No amount of discouragement could diminish his love for human beings, or his pathetic yearning for their companionship. He would abandon his play, a toothsome bone, anything, at the sound of a human footstep. He would race to the panel and there he would sit for long moments, tense with eagerness, listening and waiting. And if the voice or footstep did not materialize he would drop to the ground in a gesture of patient dejection. A friendly hand could send him into raptures of whimpering delight.

In spite of Tom's protests, I often slipped down to the sheep shed to see him, and I missed him terribly when he was eventually given to a Mexican herder to be trained. In the next few months I was so busy adjusting myself to the rigors of my first Montana winter that I forgot Bogus. He was recalled to my mind when one of our best herders, a Scot called Sandy, brought his sheep through the ranch on his way to a new camp.

I followed him to the gate when dinner was over and watched him feed his dogs. They adored him; it was easy to see that. They leaped upon him, grinning ludicrously, twisting their shaggy bodies and barking ecstatic barks.

The sight moved me to ask, 'Are herders ever cruel to their dogs?'

He turned about slowly and faced me. He had something to say that was hard for him to say. In all the years I have

known Sandy it was the one time I ever heard him criticize
another herder.

'Yes,' he replied hesitantly, 'some of them are.'

'In our outfit?'

He countered my question with another. 'Look, Missus,
will you ask the Boss to let me swop pups with the Mexican?
My pup is trained good. His ain't.'

'Bogus?'

He nodded.

'Hasn't the Mexican trained Bogus yet?'

He told me then that his camp had been near the Mexican's most of the winter; that on several different occasions
Bogus had slunk into his camp with the frayed ends of a rope
about his neck. There was something wrong; the Mexican
was abusing the dog.

'The first time he came I called him and he crept up on
his belly. When I touched him, he whimpered. He don't
whimper any more. He's used to my hand now.'

I looked at his hand as he stroked the head of one of his
dogs and I could understand why Bogus would grow used to
that hand. It was a kind, gentle hand; an understanding
one.

'But why should the Mexican tie him up?' I wanted to
know. I was still asking questions in those days.

A dark look twisted Sandy's face. 'Because for some
reason, he can't work him. I wish I knew why. He has to
drag him out on a rope every morning. I've watched him
through my binoculars! Whatever's wrong, the Mexican's
to blame; he's ruined the dog and he don't want the Boss to
know.' I plied him with questions but he refused to say
more.

I promised to talk to Tom and I did. He warned me that
a swop of dogs would only cause trouble. He explained

that each herder takes pride in his ability to train a pup; that such a swop would be a reflection upon the Mexican's efficiency. He'd sulk or quit; either event would be a nuisance. I shed some tears before he agreed to give Bogus to Sandy. When the exchange was made, the Mexican promptly quit.

It was a month before I heard any more of the dog. The sheep had been trailed to the Forest Reserve for summer grazing, when one day the camp-tender came down in his buckboard to take back another dog.

'That Bogus is gun-shy,' he announced. 'Sandy's all broke up. I thought he was going to bawl when he told me about it. He claims the Mexican's responsible . . . Anyway, he showed me a right good bullet hole on the dog's left hip. Darn fool Sandy, he's known for a month, but he kept it under his hat as long as he dared. Last night a bear got into the herd; Sandy took a shot at him and Bogus lit out like all hell was at his heels. He didn't come back till next day. The other dog couldn't hold the sheep alone and the bear finished off two lambs before the herd was rounded up.'

My heart twisted. I could picture Sandy, his loyalties torn. Loving Bogus as he did, but knowing too that if ever he needed a dog's help it was when he was forced to use his gun.

Tom's only comment to this news shocked me beyond belief. He said, 'Bring him in and shoot him.'

'Oh, no! No!' I protested wildly. 'You shan't do that, I won't have it!'

Patiently Tom tried to explain that a gun-shy dog can never be cured; that there is no place on a sheep ranch for a young dog that will not work; that the retired sheep dog is the only one which merits this luxury. There were seven of these at the ranch now — all we could care for.

'Then Bogus shall be my dog,' I announced, and nothing could change my mind.

The camp-tender brought Bogus down the next week. The dog had fulfilled all our expectations. His great body was strong and muscular and his shaggy, tawny coat held ruddy lights that glistened in the sunshine. But Bogus was not the same dog. His soft brown eyes were dark and stricken. When I tried to pet him, he sank to the ground and laid his great splendid head on his paws dejectedly. He endured my caresses but he made no response. It was Sandy he wanted . . . Sandy and no other.

The camp-tender handed me the end of a rope that was tied about his neck and warned: 'Keep him on this for a while. He'll go straight back to Sandy if you don't.'

For more than a week I tried to make friends with him, but he would have none of me. I could watch him from my bedroom window. At times he would strain his shaggy bronze-and-white body frantically against his bonds and whimper. At other times, he would huddle at the end of his rope, staring, mute and helpless, toward the mountains which hid his idol from his view. Waiting . . . with that dumb, unfathomable patience that is the heritage of sheep dogs. He ate only when hunger drove him to it . . . His coat became dull and his body gaunt.

One morning he was gone. His rope had been chewed in two. Tom said: 'That settles it. You could never hold him here, no matter how long you kept him tied. If Sandy takes him in, he'll demoralize the other dog and some day a bear or coyote will clean up the herd.'

I did not argue this time. I knew instinctively that death was the kinder thing. I could not bear the thought of that grieved, bewildered dog, lying inert at the end of a rope, waiting and watching the mountains. . . .

The camp-tender went back the next morning with instructions to do away with Bogus, and all that week remorse rode me hard. I felt that I had betrayed the dog; that I should have put up a fight for his life.

When the camp-tender came again, he brought good news — for me. Bogus was still alive. The camp-tender had made the mistake of letting the dog see his gun before he tied him to a tree. The dog had sensed his purpose. He had twisted the rope from his hand and leaped out into space. 'I think we've seen the last of him, though,' the man apologized sheepishly. 'I waited a week, and he never showed up.'

My pleasure at Bogus's escape was short-lived when I reflected that he was wandering about those mountains, bereft and disillusioned, feeling that every hand was against him. And then an even darker picture occurred to me. Perhaps he had been choked by the dangling rope that was still about his neck; perhaps he had died a long-drawn-out, horrible death from strangulation ... So much worse than a bullet — which was quick and merciful.

I went to Texas toward the end of that summer. My father was ill and I stayed several months, until he was up and about again. When I got home, they were shipping the lambs. As we drove through the field, we met the lamb drive and I stared incredulously. In the rear of the lambs a great shaggy dog raced back and forth. There was the poetry of motion in his flashing bronze-and-white body and his bark was the most ecstatic bark I ever heard.

'What dog is that?' I gasped. '*It looks like Bogus!*'

Tom grinned. 'It *is* Bogus. And the way he came back makes the darndest story you ever heard. I didn't write you, because I wanted Sandy to tell you about it.'

He stopped the car, for Sandy had spied us and was hurrying forward, grinning from ear to ear. I could not wait another moment to hear that story, so I got out and walked beside him in the wake of the sheep. It was a strange story...

Sandy told me that he, too, had worried for days after Bogus's escape. He'd been afraid because of the rope... But after a time he was sure the dog was still alive. The carcass of a ewe which he had skinned for his dogs showed unmistakable evidence of Bogus's nocturnal visits. And later Sandy had come upon the rope, caught in a low hanging branch. At last he had acutally caught sight of the dog on the crest of a rocky ridge, his shaggy body silhouetted tensely against the skyline. He had watched him through his binoculars, for more than an hour. When he tried to tell me about it, his eyes were suspiciously bright. 'The wind was just right... he could scent the sheep. He kept raising his head and filling his lungs with the smell. Seemed like he couldn't get enough of it.'

That was the only time Sandy ever saw him, but many things betrayed his nearness; a stealthy movement among tall weeds or willows; a flock of scolding camp robbers; his footprints near a waterhole... many signs that tore at Sandy's heart.

As the summer wore on and the wild flowers ceased to blossom except in the highest reaches of the Forest Reserve, Sandy had pushed his sheep upward. It was then he had encountered a she-bear and her cubs.

One of his dogs was a veteran, who knew better than to tangle with a cub. But the younger dog was not so wise. He ran onto the cubs in the underbrush and chased them to a tree. They scrambled up before the pup could reach them. One of them got too far out on a limb, lost his balance and fell to the ground, squealing shrilly as he fell.

Before the delighted pup could more than nose him, the mother bear bounded forward from a near-by clump of willows. Black fur erect, great jaws wide, she charged the pup, who lost his head and made straight for the herd of sheep, *ki-yi-ing* at the tops of his lungs.

Now Sandy was on the spot. If the bear followed the terrified pup into the herd, there would be wholesale slaughter in his flock. He drew his gun and tried to hold her. His bullet sung along her hip and she stopped short, moving her wicked head from side to side, unable to decide just who or where her adversary was.

Desperately the herder took aim and fired again. His shot went wild, but now the bear had seen him. She bellowed and braced herself for attack, her small red-rimmed eyes blazing with fury. Sandy knew that if he hoped to survive, he must get close enough to aim for a vital spot. He ran forward, tripped on a rock and fell face down on the ground. His gun was knocked from his hand. The bear was upon him before he could get to his feet or recover the gun.

'She raised her paw to finish me,' was the way Sandy put it. 'I — well, all I could do was shut my eyes...'

It was then he had heard a savage snarl and felt the impact of a wild, raging body. He could not mistake that snarl. It was Bogus's. The dog's teeth wedged for a second in the astonished bear's muzzle. She wheeled and raised her paw to crush him, but Bogus dodged. Only the tips of her claws raked his head.

Sandy was on his feet now, edging toward the gun. Bogus danced back and forth, and leaped again at the she-bear's throat. His teeth missed and hers crunched into his side, ripping the flesh and fur to ribbons. In a flash the dog twisted aside, making a flank attack, snarling, slashing, fastening his powerful teeth into anything he could reach.

The bear whirled and reared and the next time Bogus came within reach of her savage forearms, she crushed him to her breast.

Not a moment too soon did Sandy's bullet catch her between the eyes. She shuddered, a last snarl died in her throat and she sank to the ground. Sandy's voice was unsteady as he finished the story. 'Bogus was covered with blood and all tore to ribbons, Missus,' he said. 'He tried to get up but he couldn't make it. I knelt down beside him and he licked my hand.' His eyes were moist and filled with wonder. 'They say a gun-shy dog can never be cured, but he licked my hand and *I still held the gun!*'

There was so much that Sandy didn't tell; so much that my mind could supply. That splendid, battle-scarred dog, staggering to his feet and falling again. Sandy beside him ... A feeble, swollen tongue licking a beloved hand, oblivious of the fact that it clutched the thing feared most in all the world.

Bogus is gone now. He lived to a ripe old age, and he worked until he died. He was laid to rest in the small burying ground we reserve for our dogs. Some day when the sheep business warrants the outlay I shall put up a stone to his memory. Upon that stone there will be a name, and the simple phrase, '*Perfect love casteth out fear.*'

I 2

We harvest our ice

THERE is no month in the year when the woolgrower of the Northwest can conscientiously leave his work and take a lengthy holiday. Beside the four major activities of the sheepman's year, there are other important jobs scheduled to be done between breeding and lambing: the cutting and hauling of ice for summer consumption, the 'eyeing' and the 'tagging' of sheep and the preparation for lambing, which takes more time than the lambing itself.

In January or February we spend a fortnight putting up ice, stowing it away in the sawdust of the old log icehouse, which in years gone by was the Old-Timer's homestead cabin.

It takes around twenty tons of ice to supply the ranch in summer, in spite of the fact that we now have two electric refrigerators. One of these is a huge basement storage plant where beef, pork, venison and mutton are hung; the other, a smaller box, is kept in the dining-room and used for milk, butter and perishable foods.

The storage box has a freezing unit which we are unable to use because the meat requires a temperature of not more than thirty-four degrees. The ice-making capacity of the smaller box (around sixteen pounds daily) is insufficient for our needs and I'm glad it is. I may be old-fashioned, but I still prefer the crystal-clear ice cut from the lake to the cloudy cubes of modern refrigeration.

Our ice, and most of the ice in the Valley, is cut on Madison Lake, twenty-two miles from the ranch. This is one job that can never be got out of the way before the roads drift in, because there must be around two months of sub-zero weather to freeze the lake to a depth which will ensure the safety of the men who saw and load the ice, and the big trucks that haul it.

In these days when electric, gas and oil refrigeration has placed the old-time iceman on a level with the outmoded horse and buggy, it would be hard for the average city-dweller to imagine the trouble a Montana rancher takes on when he puts up his ice.

Ice-harvesting is a community project. Those ranchers who live nearest the lake test and measure the ice frequently after the first hard freeze. When word goes out that the time is ripe, snowplows clear the way for trucks in all directions. Day after day this curious parade moves slowly back and forth from the ranches to the lake.

If the roads are not too bad our own trucks can haul a load apiece each day, but I have known times when it took all of two days; times when our trucks got bogged down in drifts and had to be shoveled out by hand.

The snowplow will never replace the hand shovel in

Montana. Often a snowplow will break up the drifts, clear
the road and, its work done, be taken to the ranch. A
sudden wind blows up and hurls the snow right back into
place. The hapless motorist who attempts to pass these
drifts is forced to use his shovel.

The Treasure State owes much of her progress and prosperity to this humble farm implement. Shovels were used
first for early-day placer mining. Later shovels turned
water on miles of grazing land and transformed those miles
into fertile fields of alfalfa and grain. But, most important
of all, shovels have saved many a human life in case of
accident or illness by opening roads.

The statesmen who designed the seal of Montana gave
credit where credit was due when they placed a shovel well
in the foreground of this symbolic disk. There is no other
one implement so much in daily use. For nine months of
the year the shovel is standard equipment of every car
and truck, as much so as a jack or spare tire. No native
would dream of setting forth for even the distance of a
mile, except on state-maintained highways, without this
standby of the road. Should a newcomer forget, he seldom
forgets more than once. By the time he has floundered
through several miles of snow afoot — to the nearest ranch
or town — he has learned several things that help improve
the memory.

But the shovel reaches the climax of its usefulness in
the ice-cutting season, for as a rule the roads are then at
their worst. I have known years when the roads drifted in
so persistently that a snowplow's best efforts proved ineffectual; when the trucks have been forced to detour
through fields whose stubborn rocks would snap even the
blade of a giant steam shovel. I recall two years when we
were snowbound for a month and made no attempt to put

up ice or perform any task, except the all-important one of feeding the sheep.

I particularly remember the iceless summers that followed, for while it is always cold in morning and evening, the midday and afternoon temperatures of Montana often equal those of Texas. Iced tea is a favorite beverage with ranch men, and the lack of ice after a sweltering day in the hayfields worked a hardship on them all.

I came to Montana before household artificial refrigeration was general. The iceman had been a familiar figure in my old home, connected always in my mind with stifling heat and blazing sun — with all the discomforts of a summer in Texas. The ice harvest then was of especial significance and interest to me, but I did not have an opportunity to watch the procedure until my second winter here.

The ice was right in late January that year. I went down to the lake with Tom, and the road was open that morning. There had been little wind since the plow cleared the road the day before and we drove well in advance of the trucks. When we reached our destination we found several trucks had arrived before us. It was cold — a still, bitter cold. Someone had kindled a huge bonfire on the shore and a number of women and small children were gathered about it watching the ice-cutters now on the lake.

Sawing and loading ice is a hazardous venture, for there may be thin spots in the lake in spite of frequent testing, and one of our trucks encountered just such a spot. I joined the group about the fire and watched this same truck back cautiously, inch by inch, out on the broad expanse of snow-covered ice. At a point some fifty feet from shore, the truck stopped and two men climbed out. They unloaded a saw, a crowbar, an axe and a pair of ice tongs attached to a length of heavy rope.

One of the men chopped a hole in the ice and inserted his saw. Taking turns at the saw, the two of them shaped the ice into enormous squares weighing better than one hundred and fifty pounds each. This procedure went on for most of the morning. I was stiff with cold and becoming bored with the monotony of it before enough ice had been sawed to make up a load. But my interest revived when I saw the men lay their tools aside and lower a plank from the rear end of the truck to the ice.

One man jumped aboard, caught up the end of a rope and braced himself against the cab. His companion pried up a square with the aid of a crowbar and inserted the tongs on either side. The rope went taut and the points of the tongs took hold. One man guided the ice tongs and shoved while the other pulled until the block of ice had been drawn up the plank and into the body of the truck.

Square by square the ice was loaded and finally the job was done. I saw the ice-cutters lift the end gate to the back of the truck to secure their load, and was on the point of walking back to the car when an ear-splitting yell rang out across the lake. With one motion both ice-cutters hurled the end gate from them and made a frantic leap for safety. As I watched, I heard a sickening crackle and saw the tail end of the truck slowly break through the ice and sink into the lake.

The depth of the water at this point was close to ten feet, and in less time than it takes to tell it the truck was up-ended, with only a portion of the cab poking out of the ice. It took two days, six men, a wrecker and a block-and-tackle to right it again and eventually tow it to shore, and we were minus a load of ice when it got there.

As soon as the ice harvest is out of the way the ewes are brought, band by band, to the home ranch to be 'eyed.'

Cold weather makes wool and during the bitterest months an excessive growth forms about the ewe's eyes. The weight of the snow forces it down until it completely curtains her eyes, and unless this wool is sheared away she becomes wool-blind and can no longer see to graze or follow the herd. She gets thin and weak from insufficient feed, and so clumsy and uncertain in her movements that she is likely, at any moment, to precipitate a 'pile-up' — a calamity I shall speak of later.

After the ewes have been eyed, they are herded on the range until a fortnight before lambing, when they are again brought into the home ranch to be 'tagged' (have the loose ends of wool sheared away from teats and hind-quarters). These long, dirty ends of wool cannot be left on the ewe until she drops her lamb because flies will then blow them; maggots will hatch, work through the ewe's flesh and often bring about her death. The tags are also a menace to the newborn lamb, which will mistake them for his mother's teats, suckle them and be sickened.

Lambing lasts little more than a month, but it takes the better part of another month to get ready for it. We usually run three lambing camps, which operate from Cherry Creek, Sunrise and the Arthur Place. Each is equipped to take care of ten men and a cook. Each has its separate cookshack, bunkhouse, sheds and corrals, to which supplies and equipment of all kinds must be hauled.

None of these camps are closer than ten miles to the home ranch, and for weeks before lambing, crews of men are constantly on the road and in the camps — hauling tepees, sheep crooks, lanterns, six-foot panels, tools, dishes, kitchen utensils, fresh straw for the bunks, and stoves; ridding the buildings of mountain rats and cleaning them thoroughly; setting up stoves and tents for the overflow from the bunkhouse; clearing ditches of rubbish that has accumulated during the long winter, so that water will be plentiful for camps and sheep.

When all this work has been finally accomplished the sheep are thrown into three large drop bands, brought in to the camps — and lambing begins.

13

Lambing

THE spring chinooks have come and gone. Again and again those magic south winds have swept across the ranch, releasing the grass from winter's grip. One day hard-crusted snow blanketed the land — the next, it had vanished completely. The melting snow, unable to penetrate the frozen earth, had found an outlet in rushing, eddying streams, and water was running from every direction.

Strange winds — deceptive ones, which no native has ever been able to explain to my satisfaction. I've been told that the chinook is the indraft of a storm center; a high, dry wind that has been heated by compression in its swift descent to the lower levels.

The woolgrower has a deep respect and affection for the

chinook. It is one of his sturdiest allies, for it unlocks his grass at a season of the year when he needs it desperately, and a chinook that blows in February or March ensures green grass for May lambing.

Perhaps this is the reason that no stockman will admit its discomforts. From Tom's first description of a chinook I got the idea that it was a warm, balmy wind. Well, maybe it is when it first strikes the snow, but the moment moisture rises and water begins to run, it is bitterly cold — the sort of damp, disagreeable cold that penetrates the warmest garments and sets your teeth to chattering like castanets. I, too, am grateful for the benefits it brings, but I still know when I'm cold.

It is late May in Montana and we have been lambing for three weeks. As usual, the ranch has been a bedlam. Every man, dog, car, truck and buckboard has been pressed into active service, but in the past few days things have begun to thin out a bit, for lambing is almost over.

The drop bands (sheep to be lambed) have dwindled to one-fourth their original size, and on every hill and each grassy hollow there are small bunches of ewes and lambs which have been separated and branded according to the ages of the lambs. Later, when the lambs have been docked (had their tails burned off), these small bunches will again be thrown into the ewes' original herd and placed in the care of a herder.

In the past my contribution to lambing has consisted in the main of nothing more than errands, but there were complications this year and I got a new job. The draft and defense industries on the West Coast absorbed a number of men from this valley and we found ourselves short-handed at the start. Tom scoured the country for lambers and I did the same. Eventually we managed to gather up a skeleton crew, but it consisted largely of old men and young lads.

Lambing had no more than begun when one of these lads was inducted into the army. He'd been driving tepee truck for a drop band at Sunrise Camp. Since no one could be found to take his place, I offered to try it. The arrangement was supposed to be temporary but it did not turn out that way, and I'm glad.

Driving tepee truck is a humble job, beneath the dignity of a lamber, but it suits me fine. The ten-mile drive through the hills to Sunrise Camp is beautiful in the early morning. This is the season between snow and flowers, when the first soft green of grass and moss spreads over the hills with a promise. The long hard winter is over. Next month the ranch will be literally carpeted with wild flowers — bird's-bills, dogtooth violets, crocuses, wild irises, evening primroses and forget-me-nots — a tangled, riotous fulfillment in colors no artist could paint. Beautiful, yes, but I like this season better. For everywhere I look I can see the stir of new life — in the tender, pale green of the hills, rolling on and on to meet the horizon; in the deepening green of slender, silver-trunked quaking aspen; in the sweet, sharp-scented fragrance of pine and spruce and fir, as the sap runs through their branches.

The birds are nesting again. I see an eagle soar through the cloudless sky, wheel in midair and come to light on some rocky, forbidding peak. A curlew takes fright at the sound of my motor ... There is a plaintive cry and, fascinated, I watch the time-old trick of the curlew mother — the ridiculous pretense of a mortally wounded bird, with flapping wings and staggering, painful gait. Pathetic camouflage, distracting attention from a nest in near-by rocks. A pheasant struts out of the currant bushes and I slam on the brakes as he crosses the road, unafraid, eyeing me arrogantly, his brilliant shining head cocked on one side. And then I hear a sound that is to me the most beautiful in all the world — the liquid, golden notes of the meadowlark.

My truck rattles over the last of the hills and I look down on Sunrise Camp. The drop band is spread out below me, like a magic white carpet moving rhythmically over the green of the range. From the position of the sheep I know I'm late again; that already the herd has started out to graze. I speed up my truck, leaving the road now and bumping through sagebrush and rocks.

But once I pull up in the wake of the herd, I shall have plenty of time. Time, while waiting in the truck, to catch up on my reading and correspondence, time to chat with the herders and lambers. These conversations will not be altogether satisfactory since they are sure to be one-sided. However, I need only look around me to understand why the men who lamb this particular drop band have little time for talk.

Two-year-old ewes, lambing for the first time, are notoriously poor mothers. They're even more temperamental and skittish than the older ewes, which have learned from experience that any attempt to shed the responsibilities of motherhood will prove futile.

It is often difficult for a young ewe to give normal birth to her lamb, and having done so nothing would suit her better than to skip out and leave it to shift for itself. For speed and endurance the two-year-old ewe has most animals bested, which is bad luck for the lamber since he has to run her down, hobble her, and confine her in a small canvas tepee with her lamb until she decides to accept it.

The drop band is constantly on the move. The ewes are heavy with lamb, clumsy and unbeautiful. I drive the tepee truck slowly in their wake until a lamber signals. Then there will be a fifteen-minute halt while the lamber unloads and sets up a tepee and gives chase to an unwilling mother and her lamb.

I was perfectly content with my job until one morning last week when I climbed down from the truck and walked over to a spot where one of the lambers was 'jacketing' a lamb. I've seen this procedure many times but it has never ceased to interest me.

'Mind if I look on for a while?' I asked.

The man was one of the oldsters. He'd been with us many years at this season and I knew him well. He sat back on his heels and grinned up at me. 'Remember the first time you came out alone to see the lambing?'

I remembered all right and I grinned too, but as I stood watching him deftly skin the dead lamb and place its pelt about an orphan, I had the uncomfortable conviction that my mirth had been a mistake. His words could be taken two ways. They might have been spoken in a burst of camaraderie, or might just as well conveyed a hint that the drop band is no place for a woman to be. I wanted to believe the former, but somehow I knew better. The events of the day he mentioned stood out too clearly in my mind, and I hadn't been welcome.

I was pregnant that summer, my third in Montana, and the knowledge gave everything I did or saw a new depth and meaning. Strangely enough, the last vague fear of the country left me. I was wrapped in a safe, shining garment that nothing could dim or harm. Pain and trouble were things outside my life. For others, perhaps, but not for me. My optimism and assurance made me careless of consequences and caused Tom alarm. He told me later that the whole spring had been a nightmare for him. He never left the house that he did not worry for fear I'd do something foolish.

He clucked like a fussy old hen with one chick and I persistently ignored his clucking. But he had reason to worry. I would not listen when he insisted that I confine my long daily walks to smooth level ground, I laughed when he urged me to quit driving alone, I felt abused when he shooed me away from the corral where they were branding young colts and watched the process through a pair of binoculars from my bedroom window.

I was particularly anxious to see the lambing at close quarters that year, but I knew better than to suggest it. The year before he'd taken me out just once to a drop band and the experience had been anything but satisfactory. When I tried to follow him as he started to walk through the herd he gestured me back.

'You'll embarrass the lambers,' he said.

I caught his arm and insisted: 'If I'm not embarrassed, I don't see why they should be. I want to come.'

He shook his head and left me. For the best part of an hour I had to stand around on the outer fringe of the drop band where nothing of interest happened. I was convinced that now, more than ever, he'd refuse his consent. But I was determined I'd go, and luck was with me. Tom got a subpoena to serve as witness on a case in the district court and was forced to leave home. I got into a truck and set out immediately for the nearest drop band. Welcome or not, I stayed all afternoon, and the experience made a deep and lasting impression, for I saw birth in the raw for the first time.

Lambing is probably the most interesting phase of sheep-raising, but since that day a little has gone a long way with me. For one thing, I could never bear to see anything suffer, and a ewe in labor is tortured with pain. Her labor closely resembles that of a woman, the pains coming at regular intervals and mounting in severity. Sometimes the ordeal is long drawn out — in cases of breech presentation or the misplacement of a lamb's head — and on such occasions the lamber must come to the ewe's aid or she will die. As a general rule a sheep hates to be handled. She will struggle wildly or attempt to escape when the least restriction is put upon her freedom, but when a ewe cannot give normal birth to her lamb she knows it and welcomes the aid of a lamber as gratefully as a woman would welcome help from her physician.

The lambs were dropping fast on the afternoon I've mentioned. Climbing out of the truck I counted nine men in the herd and all of them seemed to be desperately busy. At any rate, not one of them looked up to greet me. For all the attention they paid, I might have been part of the landscape.

But I refused to be discouraged. I had come to see the lambing and I threaded my way resolutely through the herd until I stood beside a ewe which was down and quite evidently in hard labor. Her body was writhing with pain. For the first time I began to doubt the wisdom of this visit. I had a sickish feeling in the pit of my stomach and the muscles in my throat felt queer and tight.

'Hello,' I said to the lamber who was attending the ewe. He grunted but did not look up. I stood there uncertainly for a moment waiting for him to say something. He didn't.

Presently I broke the silence, which was growing strained, 'Will her lamb be born soon?' I faltered.

'Not till I take it,' he muttered, still not looking up.

I know now that the poor man was violently embarrassed, but I was too concerned over the state of the ewe to be aware of it then. 'Why don't you take it?' I cried, dismayed eyes riveted on the poor creature's twisting body. 'Oh, don't let her suffer...'

'Reckon I got to.' The outraged midwife flung me a resentful glance, knelt down, turned the lamb in its mother's womb and delivered the ewe.

The lamb lay motionless for a moment, then scrambled up on small, wobbly legs and began to blat gustily. As I watched he lowered his head and sniffed. Then his body was galvanized into sudden, frenzied action. He made a bee-line for his mother and pushed his muzzle again and again against her teats.

Wild-eyed, the young ewe leaped to her feet and made a frantic dash for freedom. But the lamber was ready for this move, for he caught one of her legs with a sheep crook and hauled her back.

Holding her thrashing body against his own he allowed the newborn lamb to suckle. When its little belly was distended with milk, the man hobbled the mother, set up a tepee, shut the two inside together and stalked sulkily away. He wasted no time explaining what another lamber later explained, that the lamb would surely have died of starvation had it not been forced on the ewe.

I moved on now and came presently to a ewe which was standing over a dead lamb, blatting pathetically. I had been there but a moment when one of the men strode up with another lamb under his arm. This lamber was co-operative, if not exactly cordial (Tom said he was plain lazy and would rather 'gab than work'). At any rate, he explained the process of 'jacketing' to me in detail.

The lamb he proposed to jacket was a twin of another

ewe which had only enough milk to raise one lamb. He let me hold the twin in my arms while he skinned the dead lamb. I watched him slit the pelt along the hindquarters, catch hold of either side, and peel it off as easily as one might take off a sweater. He shook the jacket right side out and cut the front legs several inches from the body of the pelt. Then he made a slit in each of the hind legs.

All this time the bereaved mother was objecting frantically. Her eyes blazed. She pawed the earth and raised her voice in protest. Several times she backed up and made for the lamber with lowered head, but each time he shoved her away as casually as he might have brushed off a fly. When the jacket was ready he took the lamb from my arms, poked its knobby hind legs in the rear slits, thrust its head through the neck and its front legs into the sleeves he had left on the forelegs. Then he looked over his work and set the lamb down gently on its feet.

That lamb was a fantastic sight and I broke into helpless laughter. He had two tails, and the ragged edges of the pelt about neck, rear end and legs made him look as though he were in the process of peeling. But his jacket fitted. There was not a wrinkle or a crease. It might have grown there.

Until that moment the distracted mother had been moving about restlessly — as close as she dared. But she was startled and indignant when the lamb made a rush for her teats. She backed away and would have bolted had the lamber not caught her by the leg. He had a hard time hanging on to her twisting body until the intruder found a teat. The ewe continued to be stubborn. She held her head in the air and her body became rigid and unyielding. But soon curiosity got the best of her and she sniffed ... You could see her bewilderment as she hurriedly sniffed again.

She caught the scent of her dead lamb this time. Her body relaxed and she lay still until the twin had got its fill. When the lamber released her she walked away contentedly, with the lamb frisking along at her heels.

'That doesn't seem quite fair,' I protested, 'foisting that twin on the poor thing — making her believe its her own.'

'She don't think its her own,' the lamber scoffed; 'she's just lonesome and sorry, and the scent of the jacket eases her up a bit. She'll adopt the twin now and raise it good. We can take off the jacket in a week. Tom'd lose a lot of lambs and have a heap more dry ewes if we didn't jacket.'

This lamber made a mistake when he took time to explain things to me, for I followed him around the rest of the afternoon. I watched him do several jobs of jacketing and a neat delivery in a case of breech presentation. If he was embarrassed by my presence, I failed to notice it. I was disappointed when he did not ask for a job at the beginning of the next lambing season and I often wondered why. Years later someone told Tom that he said he wouldn't work at Stonyacres if he never got a job. It seems the other lambers had teased him unmercifully. He wasn't risking another visit from the Missus (whom he confided he couldn't get 'shet' of) or some of her female kin.

I was taken aback when I heard this but I didn't resent it. I never saw the man again, yet I've always felt I'd like to thank him. He was a good talker and he knew the habits and characteristics of sheep. Until that day I had thought of sheep collectively, in terms of herd or flock. He spoke of them as individuals — as different in temperament and habits as people are different — especially ewes with suckling lambs.

Through the years a ewe's reaction to her offspring has continued to amaze me. It is so like a human mother's reaction to her child. Some ewes are the maternal type, want their lambs from the start and are devoted mothers. They are stricken with grief if their lambs die from natural causes, become lost or are destroyed by coyotes. Other ewes, the restless, frivolous type, do not want to be bothered and would leave their lambs like a shot if given the chance. These differ from the human mother, however, since they make no bones of their distaste when a suckling lamb is thrust upon them. And yet this type of ewe, if forced to take her lamb, will, in time, become devoted to it.

A human mother usually has prenatal ideas concerning her child. She may have her heart set on a blue-eyed, curly-headed baby girl, but when Fate sends her a boy with straight hair and brown eyes she accepts it complacently, and loves it at once.

Not so the ewe. She seldom gets ideas, but let her get one and it's impossible to sidetrack her — especially an older ewe. If an old ewe has given birth to twin lambs several times in succession, she takes it for granted that she should raise two lambs. Should a lambing season come when she drops a single lamb, or should one of her twins be jacketed for another ewe, she is bitter and rebellious. Several times we have had ewes of this type which went out and kidnapped lambs in order to keep up the record.

I recall one ewe which for several seasons dropped twin black lambs. She was enormously proud of them and rather queened it over the rest of the ewes. When, one spring, she gave birth to one black lamb and one white, she absolutely repudiated the white one and would have trampled it to death in her rage and disappointment, had a lamber not rescued it, and jacketed it for a ewe whose lamb had been killed by coyotes.

The frustrated mother seemed bewildered, and for days

she wandered through the herd looking over every lamb that was dropped. One morning she stood in the offing and watched a ewe drop a black lamb. Before the real mother could get to her feet the old ewe calmly took possession of the lamb and permitted it to suckle. The real mother eventually had to be thrown into the dry band (ewes which did not drop a lamb) because no matter how many desperate attempts she made to recover her lamb, the older sheep came out the winner. When the lambers became aware of the mixup it was too late to do anything about it. The lamb had accepted the wrong ewe and refused to suckle his mother. The old ewe knew what she wanted. She liked black lambs; they gave her a certain prestige in the herd and she intended to have them whether or no.

The older ewes have many peculiar quirks of character, but the most outstanding one is curiosity. They are as curious and persistently intrusive as small town gossip-mongers. The newborn lamb of another ewe never fails to attract their excited interest and this is something the lamber must guard against constantly. I've seen a bunch of old ewes barge up to a newborn lamb, when the lamber was busy elsewhere, and sniff and push and shove the little fellow until he became so weary and confused that for a time he refused to accept his own mother. Should the mother chance to be a young ewe, the situation becomes serious. When the lamb is presently driven by hunger to his mother's teats, the ewe has decided that she prefers to be free, and it takes a lot of time and energy to convince her to the contrary.

However, once the relationship has been firmly established between a ewe and her lamb, it is a beautiful and amazing thing. The ewe is the most helpless of all four-footed creatures. Nature designed her that way. She has been provided with no adequate means of defending herself or her lamb — neither teeth nor horns nor heft. The only teeth a ewe has in her upper jaw are the grinders far back in the jaw. Few ewes have horns. Their bodies are not powerful enough to trample their adversaries into submission.

But ewes are almost human in their capacity for understanding. They know their limitations. To attempt defense can mean but one thing, and that thing death. Deep-rooted in the species is a sense of caution which warns them to keep away from the thing they fear. Seldom do they take a stand, and when they do the courageousness of it is all the more splendid because of its futility.

I have known ewes to fight for their young with all the courage of a lion, to fight until death ended the unequal struggle. During the lambing season the coyotes are very active in this country. They stalk in small bunches, watching their chance for a kill. The ewe is wise. She scents danger and could easily make her escape, but it is no uncommon thing to find a badly mangled ewe near the carcass of her lamb, with the story of a supreme struggle written on the sagebrush and the rocks.

One example of the devotion that exists between a ewe and her lamb will never cease to cause me wonder and delight. This is the act of 'mothering up' which takes place when the two have been reunited after a separation. The first wholesale 'mothering up' occurs when the lambs are about a month old. At that time they are cut away from their mothers and run singly through a dodge gate to be docked. After they have been docked, and the male lambs castrated, they are again turned into the corral with the ewes.

What human mother could instantly locate her child if

it were lost among a group of fifteen hundred children, and
those children in a state bordering on panic? A ewe is
supposed to be stupid, but this is no feat for her — nor
is it any feat for her lamb.

Sheep look alike to me. I could not tell one range ewe
from another if my life depended upon it. But Tom can.
He insists that their faces and blats are as individual as
the faces and voices of people, and I've heard any number
of sheepmen and herders say the same. I'm skeptical about
their faces . . . but no one who has seen a flock 'mother up'
could doubt that their blats are distinctive.

I'm always on hand for the 'mothering up' that takes
place after docking. I wouldn't miss it for the world. I
never watch the procedure of docking but I know when it
begins — by the acrid stench of the red-hot iron as it sears
through flesh and wool; by the mounting blats of the frantic
mothers in one corral and the terrified lambs in another.
And I know when it ends — if I keep my eyes on the big
paneled gate between the two corrals.

When the docking iron has seared through the last little
tail, that gate will swing open slowly and then I shall see
a miracle in the making. A sudden stir as a sea of small
woolly heads jerk up in perfect unison . . . a rumble of
baa-a-s from the other corral. Through the swirling dust
I watch a lamb in the lead leap stiff-legged into the air —
and land running. Now they are all in motion. The spell
is broken . . . On and on they surge through that gate, like
waters that break through a dam. For a few moments the
air resounds to the chaos of frantic blats, of rushing, leaping
hoofs. And then there is quiet broken only by the rustle
of the wind through the trees, and the soft little sound of
suckling lambs. The miracle has happened . . . Each lamb
has found its mother and a pattern is complete!

14

Cooks

THERE'S a stretch of county road between the ranch and town that needs badly to be changed. Five years ago the county commissioners shifted the original course of the road to a lower level, and ever since there has been a quarter-mile that is closed to winter travel because of enormous drifts. By mid-February and sometimes earlier all cars are forced to detour through a privately owned field. This field, while fairly free of snow, has not facilitated our progress into town to any great extent, for it is literally covered with boulders which are a constant menace to the axles, crankcases and chains of our cars.

For several years it has been generally conceded that a

good road could be built through the field and that the
county commissioners were going to have to do something
about it. Each winter we fuss and stew and vow that,
come spring, we'll get up a petition and lay the matter
before them. But somehow it never gets done. It's rather
like that leaking roof in the *Arkansas Traveler*; you can't
repair it in the rain, and 'when it don't rain, it don't leak.'

We paid dearly for our part in the procrastination last
winter, for Tom had double pneumonia. In late January
he contracted a heavy cold while hunting lost sheep in a
blizzard. All too often Tom had thrown off colds by the
simple process of ignoring them. When I urged him to
remain indoors for a day or two he brushed aside my
objections and went right on with his work. But two days
later he came in from a sheep camp doubled up with a pain
in his chest. His face was crimson with fever and his voice
a hoarse rasping whisper. I got him to bed and telephoned
the doctor. Fortunately I caught him at home and he set
out immediately.

When he reached the stretch of road I've mentioned he
found he would have to detour through the field. His
car was a new model with very little clearance. He slid out
of the ruts, hung up on a rock and broke an axle. He
walked several miles to the nearest ranch and its owner
brought him the rest of the way. He was four hours en
route and all that time I was frantic with fear, for Tom
grew steadily worse. He became delirious and I had to call
on the cook and the chore boy to help me hold him in bed.
He kept muttering that he had to go back to a sheep camp
and he fought our attempts to deter him with the strength
of two men.

For five days the doctor did not leave the ranch. It was
nip and tuck with Tom. The crisis came and the doctor

brought Tom through, but each of those days seemed a thousand hours long to me. I had plenty of time to think ... Next time our luck might not hold ... Next time ... But there'd be no next time. I swore that I'd talk to the neighbors and set the petition for the new road rolling as soon as spring came.

Spring came and I had to drive tepee truck for lambing. When lambing was over I consulted the neighbors one by one. But now the weather was fair and the roads passable nobody seemed especially interested. They all agreed to sign the petition if I wanted to draw it up; it was clear, however, that they believed my efforts would prove futile.

In other years their indifference might have become infectious. It's so easy to put things off — but not this year. I had only to call up a picture of that dreadful period of waiting for the doctor — Tom's splotched crimson face, his tortured gasps for breath — and the zest for my job returned.

Drafting the petition was not quite so easy as it sounds. It was going to take high-powered salesmanship to persuade the commissioners to buy a right of way through the field, blast out and grade the new road. The argument would have to be convincing and I intended to cite specific incidences of breakage and wear and tear on all cars and trucks in the neighborhood. Eventually I got a sheaf of data together, but it needed to be assembled and boiled down into the fewest possible words.

Three times I tackled these notes and three times I was interrupted before I had fairly begun. Once I had to put my work aside to do an errand that seemed inconsequential to me.

'I can see,' I told Tom crossly, 'that I'm going to be forced to take to the hills if I get this petition rolling before snow flies again.'

'Oh, well — you won't get anywhere with it. The county hasn't enough money to maintain what roads we have. Why bother?' I stared at him. That *he* could forget...

I waited for a day of quiet and presently it came. A ditch broke one night and early next morning, armed with pick-axes and shovels, every man on the place set out to repair it. They took a lunch with them, which pleased the cook. She welcomed this period of leisure too. She was piecing a quilt for her daughter's wedding present. The time was short and she was eager to finish it. I felt sure she would let me alone.

I plugged the telephone bell grimly and sat down to my work. It was very quiet. I wrote a paragraph, read it over and ripped it impatiently out of the typewriter, replacing the sheet of paper with a fresh one. I sat there expectantly, but something had happened. I could not think of a convincing word, a phrase or a sentence. As a matter of fact I couldn't think of anything but the awful silence which was suddenly more shattering than the noon whistle at a munitions factory.

I fidgeted in my chair and told myself that I would presently warm up to my task. I didn't. An hour passed... another hour. Soon it was noon. The bell rang for lunch and all I had to show for the morning was a waste-basket full of paper.

'I pieced five blocks in my quilt this morning,' the cook boasted across the table, where she'd laid a makeshift luncheon. 'How did you make out?'

'Fine,' I lied, 'just fine.' *This afternoon it would be fine. This afternoon I'd get somewhere.*

But the afternoon was no better. I simply could not concentrate and my attention began to wander. From my window I could see so many things I wanted to do. A bed of perennials outlining the little stream which rippled by the house needed weeding badly. A hollyhock just under the window had been blown askew by last night's wind. It should be straightened and I knew where to lay my hands on a stake and a length of twine. The lawn was just right for mowing, and mowing grass has always been my favorite form of exercise. But I had to draft that petition. Tomorrow there'd be interruptions. I had to do it today.

And then, as I stared uncertainly out the window, I saw a cock pheasant strut boldly into the chickenhouse. The silence was broken by a series of wild squawks and a setting hen shot out the door. More squawks followed and another hen sailed out, shedding feathers as she flew. I raced down the stairs. When I had driven the pheasant away and persuaded the clucking, indignant hens back to their nests, I returned grimly to my typewriter.

The brief interval of action had changed everything. I could write now — if I wanted to. But I sat there trying to digest an amazing and disconcerting fact, that was all at once as clear as a bell. Quiet was the last thing in the world I needed — or wanted. Action and interruption and noise, my brain responded to these as surely as a decrepit old cavalry horse responds to a bugle. These were as necessary to me as the breath of life.

At that moment I caught sight of my shocked face in a mirror and began to laugh. I slumped back in my chair and went off into gale after gale of helpless laughter. I couldn't stop. The cook came hastily out of the dining-room and shouted up the stairs, 'What's wrong?'

'Nothing's wrong,' I choked. 'Everything's right, but it's taken me more than twenty years to find it out.' Already the wording of that petition was falling into pattern. I heard her close the door softly. She's been thinking I'm a little off for some time, and now she knows it. But everything was right ... All these weeks, trying to push back the life on this ranch, to shut myself away ... never succeeding but trying so hard. As though I could, as though I ever wanted to.

I felt like a prisoner who had unexpectedly shaken off his shackles. Worry, I told myself, never set things right. It was accepting problems and doing the best you could that solved them in the end.

There was no getting around it, I liked problems and I liked excitement and change. This knowledge left me strangely carefree and very independent. I learned something about myself that day, but I was not to learn the full extent of my freedom for another week.

At breakfast one morning a man had the bad taste to call attention to the fly he found in his oatmeal, when ranch etiquette demanded that he fish it out stealthily and conceal it on the side of his plate. I watched the cook's prompt reaction to this insult; saw her face stiffen and freeze into a solid mask of blankness, and found I didn't care.

All these years I'd been a victim of subtle blackmail, cringing before the well-known signs of a cook's impending departure — the rattle and bang of pots and pans, the impatient slam of doors. I had appeased and cajoled, and hated myself for doing it. I hadn't known it until now but, with possibly a dozen exceptions, I had welcomed a change of cooks — and the new problems they brought into my life!

I began to wonder what the next cook would be like. I've had all kinds but nothing could surprise me. There has been an ever-changing procession on this ranch since Jennie. Men cooks and women cooks, from farms and from cities. Different in manner, in disposition, in morals and in speech, but sharing one trait in common — the unfailing ability to choose the most inconvenient time to leave.

I'm a walking encyclopedia when it comes to cooks. My memory is uncanny. I doubt if there is a cook within a radius of fifty miles of whom I do not have intimate knowledge. I have their good points and their bad points at my fingertips. Through a long and painful process I have reduced the selection of cooks to a fine art. But even then Fate plays me strange tricks.

The demure, colorless little widow whom I have chosen unhesitatingly from a number of likely applicants turns out to be a bawdy woman, who boldly solicits the ranch men right under our noses. The homely, freckled-faced country girl, whose wide eyes seem to reflect an innocence that would have touched a heart less susceptible than mine, might be termed a gun moll in another walk of life. The painted, hennaed derelict, of whom I am instantly suspicious and only hire because of desperate need, turns out to be a selfless mother who is working to send her boy through school.

I have no illusions about the work in the kitchen on this ranch. Between cooks, and through part of two depressions, I've done it myself. It is back-breaking, grueling work, and exasperating as well. The dishes of one meal drag out maddeningly into the preparation of the next — the meals are never finished on schedule. There's a lot of coming and going. The irrigators and camp-tender are seldom on hand when the bell rings; Tom is frequently late. Trappers, prospectors and Rangers often drop in unexpectedly. The confusion and lack of system would try the patience of a saint.

When I first came to Montana I had had no experience whatever with white help. Our servants in Texas (Heaven help you if that word passes your lips in Montana) had always been colored. I did not know how to treat white help, and my uncertainty and inexperience resulted in those first cooks bulldozing me and getting the upper hand.

From the very start Tom made it clear that the cooks were my problem — and how glad he was to unshoulder that job. It did not bother me particularly at the time because Jennie wasn't much of a problem. Outside of being as curious as a magpie, Jennie was tops. Jennie stayed only two years, though, and when she married my troubles began.

Her successor was anxious to please. When she asked me whether I preferred liquid or dry yeast as leaven for bread, I made the mistake of saying, 'I don't know a thing about bread-making.' Now, I could just as easily have said: 'I have no preference. Use whichever you like best,' and I should have gained her respect and approval. When later in the day she felt me out again with 'Shall I scrub on my hands and knees, or can I use a mop?' I replied: 'Use the mop. That's easiest, isn't it?'

If she had been in doubt before, she had my number then, and from that day on the easiest way was the only way. She opened cans when she could have used garden vegetables. She cooked up huge quantities of food and warmed it over until it was tasteless. She begrudged us every extra plate, knife, fork or spoon that added to the burden of dishwashing. I stood it all until she suggested that we take soup on our dinner plates and then I balked, and dismissed her on the spot.

I hunted a cook for three weeks between dishwashing and scrubbing and baking, and I had learned a thing or two about ranch cooking before I got out of the kitchen. I was a strange-looking sight as I welcomed the new cook — a mass of cuts and burns from my fingertips to my shoulders, which gave the new cook my number. She took one look at my battle-scarred members and decided she could get away with murder. She sailed right in and bossed me out of the kitchen.

She gave me to understand from the start that she didn't like a woman messing around. She was frank to admit that she had hoped to land a job with a bachelor or a widower, because men never interfered with her work. But women, now women were the dickens. Always getting underfoot and snooping . . .

She wasn't a good cook. Her pastry was terrible and the meat she baked was either gray and limp and underdone, or burnt to a crisp. But if I so much as bleated a feeble remonstrance she hinted dourly that there were plenty of jobs, better jobs, waiting for her. They didn't wait long. I began to look for another cook, but I had learned one bitter lesson, and I hunted secretly. I had another woman ready to step into her shoes before I gave notice.

That woman arrived with twelve canaries in a half-dozen cages, and she left in a huff the next day because I refused to let the chore boy bore holes for the cage hooks in the plastered ceiling of her bedroom.

The next cook was a Charmer. She was frankly on the hunt for a man, and having picked out the object of her affections, an irrigator, she showered him with delicacies and attention. His slice of pie was always at least two inches bigger than any other slice on the table. Flapjacks disagreed with him, so we seldom had flapjacks. He liked weak coffee, and we liked it strong, but we had weak coffee.

This state of affairs did not find favor with the men, so they took it out on the irrigator. There was bickering and ill feeling in the bunkhouse. Eventually the irrigator rebelled, turned over his shovel and boots and asked for his time. And he took the Charmer with him.

I was fed up with women cooks by this time and in desperation I hired a man. He was an ex-prospector, a quiet, affable man and a very good cook. He stayed two years, until he accumulated enough money to work a claim he'd staked out. Encouraged, I hired another man, who turned out to be anything but satisfactory, since he was drunk half the time.

Five cooks came and went before we found one that was possible. This woman was not as neat as she might have been but she was a good cook and she made the best bread I ever tasted. It was snow-white, even-grained and surprisingly light. She held down her job for six months on the strength of that bread. The men were crazy about it and lavish in their praise. I shut my eyes to a slight frowsiness of hair and dress, an untidy kitchen and an occasional half-washed plate, because a ranch cook who can make good bread is a jewel beyond price.

One day, at table, I noticed a peculiar tension. There was little talk and no praise for the cook. Furthermore, none of the men seemed hungry, and when the bread plate was passed it went from hand to hand so quickly that it might have been red-hot. Not one man took a slice. Puzzled, I looked my piece over and tasted it. It seemed all right; if anything it was lighter and more palatable than usual.

The moment the meal was over I cornered the chore boy and asked him what was wrong. He told me that the cook, that morning, had explained to him the secret of her excellent bread. She slept with the sponge to keep it warm.

In spite of the queer things that have happened here, the best, most loyal friends I have on earth are some of the women who have cooked for me. Whatever their backgrounds, they are gentlewomen in the truest sense of the word.

With profound love and gratitude I think of Hazel, a young girl who worked for us when our two sons Leigh and Andy were quite young and our next baby soon to come. The boys were at an age to be a handful. They were into everything and for several months I was too sick to know, or hardly care, what they did.

We were desperately hard up that summer. It was nip and tuck to make ends meet. There had been a drought two summers before and the hay crops that were harvested turned out to be only fifty per cent of normal. The range was sparse and scorched. The outlook was black as we went into the winter, and little did we guess how black. It was a winter that no Montana stockman cares to remember. By November 1 the thermometer had plunged down to forty below zero; the snow was eighteen inches deep and still piling up. There was no chance whatever of the sheep pawing through to the grass, which was sparse enough at best.

The preceding winter hay could be bought for seven dollars and a half a ton, but that tragic year it soared in price to forty dollars and was alarmingly scarce at that. Tom was unable to buy enough in our valley and had to trail his sheep to the Ruby Valley, which was thirty-eight miles over a high range of mountains.

That winter our sheep were fed from November until April on hay that cost forty dollars a ton. In dollars and cents Tom paid more to winter his ewes than he could possibly have sold them for the following fall. And to add to his troubles the price of wool and lambs took a terrific slump. With my usual lack of foresight I seemed to have picked exactly the wrong time to add to our family, for things got steadily worse. If ever Tom needed my help he needed it then. There were numberless things I could have done to ease the weight of his burden, but for months each time I raised my head from the pillow the room whirled around and wave after wave of nausea took hold of my body.

During this time Tom was cutting corners everywhere and doing the work of two men. Every ranch wife I knew had discharged her cook. And there I lay. There was no money to pay a cook and I knew it. Tom had even borrowed on his life insurance to meet the wages of the men.

For some eight months before the girl Hazel came to the ranch, I'd been doing the cooking myself. When I became pregnant and was unexpectedly ill Tom went into Butte and brought Hazel home. As usual he asked no questions — just took her on faith.

I liked the girl's looks when I saw her first. She was a big strapping girl, with a broad, pleasant face, candid blue eyes and a friendly smile. But she had not spoken a dozen sentences before I felt I simply couldn't have her around. For one thing her voice was rasping and loud. It tore at my sick nerves. I could have taken that in my desperate need, but she'd been cooking in a rough mining camp and the background of her previous job had not improved her vocabulary. She swore like a mule-driver. Her conversation was interspersed with 'I told them what the hell — I want a job with a family . . . where they've got kids,' or 'You never saw such a god-damn mess in your life.'

Leigh and Andy were all too ready to pick up rough talk and I shuddered to think of the example she'd set them. I smile — remembering. The day was to come when no strain of haunting music could give such comfort to my soul as Hazel's raucous voice — god-damns and all.

I was racking my brain for some excuse to let her out easily when she started telling me about her past life.

She'd been raised in a state institution for orphans, she said, had never had any folks of her own ... She loved the country and she loved 'kids.' She told her story simply, making no bid for my sympathy, but just the same there was a wistfulness about it that struck deep into my heart. I let her stay.

Hazel turned out to be a model of efficiency and understanding. She kept the whole house as neat as a pin. She was a good, economical cook, and her kitchen ran on greased wheels. She turned out her work quickly and even found time to do the laundry. And best of all, she adored the boys. She took them off my hands and managed them so beautifully that I scarcely knew they were around. But she disciplined them. They had an immense respect and affection for her. I recall a conversation I overheard between Leigh, our oldest boy, and Hazel.

'Leigh! What's that you said?' Hazel's voice rolled up the stairs with the volume of an off-key bass fiddle.

'I said "What the hell,"' Leigh sang out.

'Well, don't you say that again.'

'You say it,' he accused.

'And I'm going to go right on saying it. But you're not. You hear me?'

He heard and he heeded.

Hazel knew how hard conditions were. Anyone would have known. There was tragedy in the air — a question in everyone's eyes. Shearing was coming up soon. It took cold cash to meet that heavy additional expense — and where was it coming from? In our case it came from a mortgage on the land.

For the first and only time Tom was forced to place a mortgage on the ranch. He hated to tell me. He tried so hard to convince me that it was the proper, normal thing to do. It was only a small mortgage, he said, which would be paid off after the lambs were shipped. He meant to sound casual — to leave the impression that he thought nothing of it — but he couldn't fool me. I knew what it took of his courage — how deeply it wounded his pride.

Our sheep had already been mortgaged to the last dollar of their value, but that was different. Sheepmen expect to mortgage their sheep for current running expenses. Chattel mortgages can be paid off in the fall. This is customary. But not the land — the land is the woolgrower's roots. And a man without roots ... It was the last, desperate stand, and I knew it.

I was stricken, though I, too, tried not to show it. My mind twisted and turned but it always came back to the fact that I wasn't carrying my share of the load. Tom was shouldering it alone. I thought of all the sacrifices the women around me were making. I could think of no ranch woman who had not let her cook go — and most of them were doing their laundry as well. I told myself miserably that I had to do something about it. In spite of the doctor's orders, I meant to get out of bed. I meant to let Hazel go.

I didn't tell Tom. I knew he'd never agree, and I waited until he'd left the house before I called Hazel. I explained as gently as I could, but she stared at me, hurt and indignant, and refused to leave. Moved to tears by her loyalty I nevertheless insisted. 'You'll have to go,' I said. 'Don't you understand, Hazel? — We haven't the money to pay you.'

Her face cleared up. She dropped down on her knees beside my bed and put her strong young arms around me. 'Pay?' she scoffed. 'Hell — who wants any pay? I'll work for my board — and damn glad to. You're all the

folks I've got and you need me. The kids need me. Sick
as you are, Leigh and Andy'd worry you into your grave.
Then where'd the Boss be, left to herd those two young
devils alone?'

I told her that that set-up wouldn't be fair to her. She
was a good cook and could make good wages elsewhere.

'I wouldn't be good anywhere if I was worrying about
you and the kids,' she announced firmly, and dismissing the
matter, she hurriedly left the room.

Hazel stayed with us four years, in fact until she married. She helped me through that ghastly summer, she took
excellent care of Tom and the boys that fall when our
daughter Louise (Wezie) was born. And she worshiped
the baby. I didn't regain my strength for months after my
return from the hospital, and I often wonder what I should
have done without that blessed girl.

She begrudged every moment spent away from Wezie.
Each morning she'd carry her bassinet down to a sunny
corner in the dining-room so she could be near her as she
worked. At night she carried the bassinet reluctantly back
to the nursery. Many times, on bitterly cold nights, when
I was on the point of going to see if the children were covered, I'd hear Hazel creeping softly up the stairs to make
sure. Where Wezie's welfare was concerned, she wasn't
trusting anyone, not even Wezie's mother.

Next year the sheep business came into its own again.
The lean cycle gave way to a time of prosperity and we
watched the price of lambs and wool soar. We paid off our
debts. But there was one debt we didn't pay. We didn't
even try. We still owed Hazel six months' wages. You
can't pay for love and loyalty with dollars and cents — and
we knew it.

When Hazel was married we gave her a check far in

excess of her back wages. She didn't want to take it. She turned it over in her hand and glared at it suspiciously.

'You're trying to pay me for those six months I worked for my board,' she brought out stiffly. 'It's not fair and I don't like it.'

Tears stung at my throat. I wanted to break down and bawl. I caught her arms and made her look at me. The clear candor of her eyes accused and reproached.

'Hazel,' I choked. 'You blessed, blessed fool...'

'I don't like it,' she repeated stubbornly.

I was ready for this. I had known it was coming. 'Hazel,' I asked, 'what would you say Wezie was worth in dollars and cents?'

Her face lighted up and her honest blue eyes sparkled, '*Wezie!* Hell — there's not enough money in the mint to pay for Wezie.'

'Child, don't you know that you gave her to me? I could never have carried her nine months if you hadn't been here. The doctor said so. There can never be any talk of *pay* between us... It has to be give and take.'

She was uncertain for a moment, and very thoughtful... wrestling with the problem. And then I could see that she was pleased. She grinned, folded the check and placed it carefully in her pocket. We were her folks again.

I 5

Shearing

A FEW months ago I was sorting out some old letters and papers and I ran across a composition which Wezie had written in the second grade of school. It was brief and to the point and its subject was *Shearing*. I showed it to Tom and we laughed together over the sprawling misspelled words. The first sentence is a masterpiece and it sums up shearing aptly:

> *Shearing is a lot of truble to make pretty sheep ugly aspeshally if it rains.*

This sentence may convey little to the outsider but it will strike a responsive chord in the heart of every woolgrower who reads it.

I have thought about that composition a number of times in the past three weeks, but I haven't felt like laughing. Our shearing is just finished and it dragged out interminably because of rain. It's queer — drought may harass us for months on end, but once we start shearing the skies will open up and give forth in torrents. I've seldom known it to fail. Rain, so welcome in this country at any other season, is a bugaboo at shearing time.

The weather was fair the day we started. The sun blazed down on the tar-papered roof of the shearing pens at Sunrise. Wave after wave of sweltering heat rose on clouds of dust and mingled with the hoarse shouts of the wranglers, the staccato barking of dogs and a chorus of frantic *baa-a's*. The unsheared ewes in the corrals panted for breath. Inside, the shearers were stripped to the waist and sweat glistened on their chests and arms and rolled in little rivulets from their faces. The water boy raced back and forth with his canvas-covered bottle, stopping frequently so all could slake their thirst. It was too hot to breathe in comfort, yet everyone was happy. This was proper weather for shearing. If it lasted, the job would be done in four more days.

It didn't last. On the morning of that second day the skies were overcast and there was a hint of rain in the air. The shearers worked doggedly against time, their shining blades flashing in and out of the fleeces of wool with incredible speed and precision.

By mid-afternoon the thunder was rumbling ominously behind the mountains to the south and jagged streaks of lightning ripped through the dun-colored clouds like scissors of flame. The air was strangely still and oppressive. And then the storm broke and the rain came. Sheets and sheets of it ... pelting the dusty corrals, running in streams across the parched grass of the range, and soaking through the fleece of every sheep not under cover.

As the rain settled to a steady downpour the tempo in the shearing pens decreased. The blades of the shearers moved slowly. The water boy hung his canvas bottle on a nail and looked out on the storm. The wranglers turned all dry sheep into the pens and lounged about, rolling cigarettes in leisurely fashion. Even the dogs sought the shelter of the shed and stretched out on the floor. Work was almost over for the day — and the next day, perhaps. Everybody knew it. It would take a good six hours of wind and sun to dry out the sheep that got caught in the storm. Wet wool can't be sacked because it will mold. There would be no more shearing until the sheep were dry.

In the three weeks that followed this first rain, we got in only a few hours of shearing each day. The weather followed a definite pattern — mornings of sun and warm drying wind, and afternoons of rain.

Our shearing pens are situated in the center of a vast flat, ten miles from the home ranch. The flat is surrounded on all sides but one by low hills which mount in gentle grassy slopes to the timbered mountains. During shearing our entire flock grazes on these hills. One herd at a time they are brought down to the sheds, corralled and separated from their lambs. Since this separation should not exceed six hours — for the welfare of both ewe and lamb — only a small per cent of ewes can be kept under cover for any length of time.

The area surrounding the shearing sheds, cookshack and bunkhouse resembles a small tent city, for we employ a crew of between thirty-five and forty men. This crew consists of shearers, herders, wranglers, wool-tiers, branders, trucksters, a 'tromper' (sacker), a tallier, a weigher and a water boy.

Most of the shearers in this country belong to itinerant crews who follow the season from state to state. These crews start their trek north in January from California and Arizona and work up through Nevada, Utah, and Idaho, reaching Montana sometime in July. As a rule there are from twelve to sixteen shearers, two wool-tiers and a captain in each group.

The captain's word is law. He maps out the work and arranges for the various jobs on approximate dates (subject, of course, to fair weather). He takes care of the financial end of the deal and bargains with woolgrowers by telephone, wire or letter well in advance of the job. He shears along with his crew but also supervises their work and settles disputes.

The captain is the buffer between the sheepman and the shearer. A careless shearer, nicking too large a percentage of sheep, is reported to the captain, who handles the situation — sometimes by tactful persuasion; sometimes with his fists.

For his supervision and discipline he receives a certain per cent of each shearer's earnings, which nets him a tidy sum, since the average shearer makes between twelve and fifteen dollars a day.

Machine shearing has replaced blade shearing in many states, but the veteran woolgrower of Montana still prefers the blade. He contends that the machine shaves the sheep instead of shearing them, and it is true. The motor-driven clipper penetrates to the very flesh of the ewe, while the hand blade leaves a good half-inch of wool on the back. This wool serves as protection from the blazing summer sun, which frequently blisters the tender exposed flesh of the ewe which has been shorn by machine. In time — according to the veteran — close shearing and resultant blistering will retard the growth of new wool and even lower its quality. The patrons of hand shearing also contend that the ewe which has been machine-sheared goes into the winter with insufficient wool to repel the cold and driving snow, and suffers from exposure as a consequence.

I'm no defender of the hand-blade crew — I know the machine crew is faster. But I am a staunch defender of the traditions of this country. I should hate to see the old, intimate, colorful customs give way to the impersonal efficiency of modern-time machines. And they are doing just this. More and more the younger generation of woolgrower is leaning toward machine shearing. Each year this method has its converts. I can see the handwriting on the wall. But this I know: the flocks at Stonyacres will always be shorn by hand so long as Tom is master.

The shearers are paid on the basis of so much per head for sheep sheared (of late years between twelve and fifteen cents). The balance of the crew, with the exception of the herders, are paid only for the days they work. But all must be fed regardless, and while the enforced vacation — a result of bad weather — may affect the dispositions of the crew, it certainly does not affect their appetites. They eat three square meals a day at the woolgrower's expense and there's nothing he can do about it.

Continued rain gets on everyone's nerves. The shearers and wool-tiers are restless and short of temper. They feel confident that the weather is fair on the other side of the mountain where another job awaits them, and worry lest their next employer may become impatient over the prolonged delay and pick up an idle crew, thus curtailing their own earnings for the season.

The herders are cross because the sloping hills do not afford the best grazing in the world and too long a delay will result in serious shrinkage of ewes and lambs. For a full year the herders have lavished time and care on their flocks with no chance to display the result of their efforts. They've looked forward to shearing, each confident that his will be the prize herd of the outfit. What use all this trouble if rain steals their thunder?

The woolgrower is edgy and silent. He has reason to be. Each pound his flock shrinks cuts into his profits, and the expense of feeding an idle crew mounts to alarming proportions with every day lost.

Before I came to Montana the very word *shearing* called up a fascinating picture in my mind — of milling, bleating herds which moved in perfect harmony to the shearer's blades. I supposed the act of shearing was accomplished with rapidity and ease, and it never occurred to me that a flock of fat white ewes could emerge from the pens huddled, shrunk to what appeared half their former size, with what remained of their lovely soft wool transformed to a hideous dingy brown.

I remember so well the first bunch of shorn sheep I ever saw — my dismay and disillusion. The wranglers were turning them out of the branding chute into the corral to mother up with their lambs. I sat in the car and stared with much the sensation I should have experienced had a flock of picked cold-storage chickens suddenly flapped their wings, raised naked heads and begun to crow. I decided in that moment that there was nothing glamorous about shearing and I've never changed my mind. But it's an interesting procedure if you can shut your eyes to a few things like the bloody gashes made by careless, impatient shearers, or the accidental amputation of a ewe's ear or teat. I've never seemed able to do it.

There are sixteen pens in our shed, and these pens are flanked on either side by long narrow alleyways which run the full length of the building. The sheep to be sheared are wrangled down the alleyway to the right into the pens. As each sheep is shorn her fleece is kicked by the shearer into the alleyway on the other side, where a tier rolls it into a compact bundle, ties it securely and tosses it up to the 'tromper.'

The wool-tromper is a hero, and the pay and a half he receives doesn't begin to compensate him for the hardest, hottest, most disagreeable job at the sheds. The wool-tromper is usually a permanent employee of the outfit, who has the job forced upon him. He is always easy-going and good-natured or he would never permit himself to be so put upon.

I recall one tromper who, during shearing, just missed being struck by a rattlesnake. The reptile was coiled in the underbrush between the cookshack and bunkhouse. It struck but its deadly fangs glanced harmlessly off the side of the tromper's boot. When he showed me the exact spot on the top of his boot I said: 'That was cheating death with a vengeance. Another inch and he'd have got the calf of your leg. Weren't you afraid?'

'Afraid!' He threw back his head and shouted with laughter. 'And me tromping thousands of pounds of wool every day? Say, Missus, there's nothing on the Other Side that could be worse than tromping wool on a hot summer day!'

I was inclined to agree with him. Wool-tromping was not my idea of an easy, pleasant job!

A wool sack around seven feet long is hung down a narrow shaft from an elevated platform and secured at the top by a circular hoop, which fits snugly into the floor of the platform. The sack clears the ground by a foot and the tromper must tramp his way from the bottom of the sack to the top. He is almost suffocated by the dusty, foul-smelling fleeces. He is choked and blinded but can get no relief until he has tramped the wool to a height where he can poke his head over the top of the sack. Before he has tramped his first sack his face and body are plastered with wool grease that has caked with dust and he smells to the heavens.

When the sack has been tramped full enough (three hundred and fifty to four hundred pounds, depending upon the will-power and lungs of the tromper), the weigher is signaled and he pries the sack up on a pole and balances it until the tromper can release the top from the encircling hoop and sew the sack.

The sack is then tripped and turned over to a weigher, who rolls it to the scales and stencils the number of pounds and the owner's name on the burlap. It is later loaded on a truck and the sacks are hauled, several tons at a time, to a warehouse at the shipping point, where they are stored until sold.

As the sheep are wrangled out of the small pens a tallier counts and marks their number on a card which is nailed to every pen. This is the only record kept of the shearer's work, and Heaven help the tallier if his arithmetic is faulty. His job depends upon his tactfulness and accuracy. I remember one tallier who forgot to mark up six ewes. He was a cocksure fellow, and when the shearer accused him, he made the mistake of defending his figures belligerently. I took the tallier to the doctor's office when the difference of opinion had been settled, and his bashed-in face was not a pretty thing to see.

After the freshly shorn sheep have been wrangled out from the small pens, tallied and sent down the long alleyway to the branding chute, their cuts are doctored with sheep dip, and the brand of their herd is plainly marked on their backs with waterproof paint. When a complete herd has been branded the ewes are turned into the corrals with their lambs to mother up before setting out for their grazing areas.

16

Follow the signs

I SHALL never be skilled in reading Montana sign lore, and that is one of the reasons I'm still considered a tenderfoot. I've tried — I worked hard at it before I'd admit that it was above the level of my intelligence. I did master the simpler, most obvious signs, but the finer shades will always escape me.

Tom says I can't learn because I keep my head in the clouds, that I'm looking at sunsets and rainbows when I should be looking at grass and rocks and earth. This shortcoming of mine disappoints him. I see just enough to arouse his curiosity and let him down on detail which would piece out a story for him.

For instance, I know when I open the gate on my way

home from town that some car has been through since I
came out. I can't help but see that tracks cover mine in the
dust or snow. I usually know, too, that the driver was a
man because the latch is difficult and no woman could jam it
so firmly into place.

I've tactfully mentioned its peculiarities to Tom a
number of times, hoping something would be done about it.
I'm always running behind schedule, and it's annoying to
be held up within three miles of the house, stewing over a
latch that any man could fix in fifteen minutes. When I
took the skin off my fingers manipulating it the other day, I
saw red.

'Some man jammed the latch on the red gate again,' I
told Tom, 'and I skinned my hand. If you don't have that
latch repaired soon, I'm going to. It's a disgrace...'

He ignored the cause of my ill-temper and asked with
interest, 'Which way was the car headed?'

'I don't know,' I was forced to admit.

'It couldn't have been Mr. Thayer,' he speculated.
'There's a boot on the left rear tire of his pick-up. You'd
have seen a bulge in the dust every few feet.'

I wondered if I should, and I fervently hoped no bulge
had been there, for then I should have no defense. I knew
all about that boot. I'd taken the tire to the garage for Mr.
Thayer a few days before. The mechanic had explained the
amount of repair to me and I had passed the information on
to Mr. Thayer when he stopped by to pick up his tire.

Even though I know some of the signs myself I still love
to hear the natives figure things out — especially Mr.
Thayer. Our neighbor never wastes subtle yarns getting
his points across to me. If my views agree with his, he
seems disappointed; if they don't, he tries to convince me,
and he can cram more facts into fewer words than anyone I
know.

Last fall I was separating and transplanting my tulips when Mr. Thayer drove up to the gate. He'd come to tell us that we had a telephone pole down in the field. He delivered the news and stood watching me uncertainly for a moment.

I knew what he had on his mind. This was no fall to be transplanting, but I'd neglected my tulips the year before and the bulbs were far too thick. If left as they were, they'd surely die. Transplanted, they might not survive the kind of winter all signs presaged, but that winter had not come yet; I was still optimistic. I knew better than to voice my optimism, so I went right on with my digging.

Mr. Thayer did not leave. When he could stand it no longer he said: 'We're going into a hard winter. Them bulbs'll be dead come spring.'

He was probably right and the knowledge made me contrary. 'The weather's been glorious so far,' I reminded him.

'What if it has?' he exclaimed bluntly. 'All signs point to an early, bad winter. Don't you know the crows have been flocking for weeks? And the mountain rats are already making their nests? You ain't seen a gopher for days but I bet you've seen deer and elk. They're already down from the high ridges. We chased two elk out of our grain stubble only yesterday.' Now he'd warned me. If I didn't take heed, it was my bad luck. He turned and strode away.

Sign lore always sounds so simple when the natives explain it, but the natives were born with the woodcraft of an Indian and the tracking instinct of a bloodhound, and I wasn't. Tom's knowledge of sign lore is positively uncanny and, curiously enough, it stops short at our door. I'm the one who can locate missing things in the house. After he has dug through closets and files with the zeal of a puppy unearthing a bone, I can lay my hand infallibly on the ob-

ject of his search. But I always let him hunt first. In this
way I manage to keep my self-esteem. It comes in handy
when I've flunked some sign of the range.

Even the most commonplace signs, the ones I've managed
to master, are confusing to the newcomer. Today I could
understand and be amused by incidents that made no sense
when I first came to Montana. For example, one day years
ago Tom and I were riding the range and we met up with
Mr. Thayer on horseback. He hailed us and said: 'You're
going to be madder'n a hornet when you ride on a piece.
My sheep's been trespassing on your lambing sections.'
And then he burst forth into vitriolic abuse of his herder.
The man was no good, didn't have the sense of a locoed
ewe...

'I met the darn fool five miles out on the flat,' he ex-
ploded. 'He'd lost his sheep. "How come you're headed
this way, then?" I asks him. He says, surprised like, "I'm
hunting my sheep." "Good God, man!" I yells at him.
"Don't you know which way the wind is blowing? If you
don't, it's time you threw a piece of paper into the air and
found out." I turned him back into the wind and sure
enough we found the sheep on your land.'

Tom laughed. He got the point, that the herder had been
hunting his sheep against a high wind, with no chance of
finding them. But I didn't. Mr. Thayer's words had no
meaning for me.

The way the people of this country read signs into rocks,
grass, wind, earth, trees, beasts and birds is amazing. It
surprises me as much today as it ever did. I've heard the
process of reasoning and seen its unerring results many
times when our sheep have strayed, but the method of
tracking is seldom the same.

I had lived here a year before I got in on a sheep hunt. Tom was not enthusiastic about taking me then. I was still a poor horsewoman and far from an adventurous one. My heart sank into my boots each time my horse went into a gallop, and Tom knew it. He warned me that I'd have to keep pace with him if I went, or turn back alone. I'd been thinking this very thing a moment before, had all but decided to stay home, but his words stung my pride. I determined to go, and to stick, if it killed me.

It was early September and shipping time. The lambs had been cut away from their mothers on the Forest Reserve. They were half-weaned, fractious and hard to keep in the fold. Halfway down the mountain the drive ran into a dense fog and the men and dogs went through a harrowing hour before they came out into the sunshine again. They were convinced that some lambs had broken away in the fog, but could not make sure until late afternoon when they reached the counting corrals near the boundary of the Forest. The lambs were corralled and counted then, and more than a hundred were found to be missing.

There's a telephone at the counting corrals and word was got to Tom. It was too late to start searching that day but we started out before daybreak next morning — Tom, two ranch men and I. We met the drive soon after sunup and learned the exact place they had run into the fog. It took three hours of steady climbing to reach this place and I regretted my decision to come along before we got there. I was already saddle-sore and weary, and the hunt had only begun.

The fog area had started in a patch of timber. The men dismounted, looked the ground over carefully, consulted and decided to separate.

Tom and I jogged along for perhaps an hour and came

presently to a barbed-wire fence. He got off his horse then, squatted back on his heels and examined the lower wire of the fence. When he came back to his horse, he said: 'There's a gate somewheres around here. We'll have to find it. The lambs came under this fence and headed north.'

I had to laugh. He was so serious and matter-of-fact. 'Did they leave you a map?' I wanted to know.

'They left a hundred.' He was in no mood for levity as he pointed to the fence. For the first time I noticed tufts of wool which clung raggedly to the lower wire. 'It's lamb's wool,' he explained. 'Its color and grease show it hasn't been off the pelt more than twenty-four hours.'

'Did the condition of the wool tell you which way they were going?' I asked as he swung into the saddle. (Even this would not have surprised me.)

'The grass and weeds did. They're trampled to the north.'

We found the gate and rode for an hour before we came upon another clue. When Tom dismounted, I got off and limped stiffly along beside him. The lambs had skirted a tangle of underbrush. 'They're still headed north,' he announced, calling my attention to hoofprints on the soft earth of a molehill, and to the outer branches of underbrush which had been grazed bare. 'But they're slowing down now. We should come on another clue soon.' We did — in less than fifteen minutes. As we rode down into a sheltered coulee even I could tell that the lambs had lingered for a time. There were sheep droppings all around. Tom said they had bedded there the night before.

Our hunt ended as the sun slipped down behind the mountains. It seemed hours since our noonday sandwich, and I had begun to have uncomfortable visions of spending a night on the trail, sans bed and food, when Tom reined in his horse on the crest of a hill, took out his binoculars and stared fixedly into space for a moment.

'Look' — he handed me the binoculars and pointed toward a narrow gulch which must have been three miles away. 'They're over there. Dead. A pile-up, most likely.'

He wheeled his horse and started off in a gallop. My horse almost leaped out from under me and followed so swiftly that the question I had been on the point of asking congealed in my throat. For the next half-hour my concern was riveted on other things — hanging on to a valuable pair of binoculars (which Tom had thoughtlessly left in my hands), the reins and the saddle-horn at one and the same time, and remaining erect in the saddle.

'What makes you think they're dead?' I gasped when we finally slowed up for a sharp rise this side of the gulch.

'The magpies and crows,' he answered grimly.

I raised my eyes and saw that the sky was full of whirling, soaring birds which set up a hideous burst of chatter as we drew nearer. When our horses had climbed to the brink of that little gulch, we looked down on a gruesome sight. There had been a pile-up and out of that hundred-odd lambs we counted fifteen still alive. These had skipped down from the top of the pile-up to make way for the scavenging birds, and were grazing unconcernedly near-by.

Fortunately the hours of daylight are still long at this season, for it was close to nine o'clock before we reached our Forest allotment and corralled the rescued lambs. We slept, that night, in the camp-tender's narrow bunk at the head-quarters camp. I woke a wiser, if lamer, tenderfoot, and never again have I had the slightest desire to take part in a hunt for lost sheep beyond the boundaries of our ranch.

The use of this sign lore, of course, is not confined to

sheep. It applies to everything that walks, crawls or flies. It even applies to Man. I remember one horse-thief who was tracked down and picked up after three days of riding, with mighty little effort on the part of the riders.

This thief had been operating in the vicinity for a month before it was determined that the horses had been stolen and not strayed. One morning the son of a neighbor rode over in great excitement and asked Tom to let him have a couple of riders to help round up the thief. He had telephoned the county seat and, unable to locate the sheriff or his deputy, had decided to take the law in his own hands before the trail became cold. Tom knew the boy's father was away from home shipping his cattle, and he also knew that the lad was hot-headed, impulsive, and given to snap judgment.

'Hold on, son,' he remonstrated. 'Your horses may have strayed. I lost two mares on the Forest last summer but I found them again in the fall. You'd better do a little more riding and make sure your horses are gone before you start out to look for a thief.'

'They are gone, and they didn't stray,' the lad exclaimed heatedly. 'They were pastured near Morgan Gulch. I picked up their trail and followed it up to the head of Ruby Creek. There were nine unshod horses in the bunch, *and one shod horse was driving them.*'

That settled the matter. Tom asked no more questions and sent two of our men to join in the hunt. They tracked those horses forty miles back into the mountains and found them in an abandoned homestead corral, along with six other horses. They lay in wait for the thief and picked him up as he attempted to drive two unbranded colts into the corral.

This man-hunt left a vivid impression with me. It was

so foreign to anything I'd ever known. As a matter of fact it
was also unusual here, but I had to learn that. Only twice
in all these years have I heard of horse-thieves operating
in the Valley. The second occasion I remember with humil-
ity because it snatched away any claims I may have had to
courage.

Tom was in Idaho at the time, buying ewes. The sheriff
called me one afternoon and asked me to have the horses
turned out of our corrals that night and to telephone my
neighbors to do likewise (as though I need telephone!).
Two horse-thieves were headed this way. He went on to
explain that a posse had run them down, recovered a dozen
horses, but the thieves had made their escape. Their general
direction was checked — always a day too late — because
the thieves rode their horses until they played out and then
helped themselves to fresh mounts from various ranch corrals. The line was tightening, the sheriff told me, and he
figured if no horses were available they'd soon be afoot and
easily captured.

The sheriff was famed for his knowledge of sign lore, so
the ranch men made no objections when I delivered his message, even though it meant they'd have to round up the
work horses again before breakfast next day. I made a mistake when I told the cook, though. She was already afraid
of her shadow, and she got as nervous as a witch. I had a
terrible time persuading her to go to bed that night. She
wanted to sit up with all the lights on, and insisted that I
keep her company. I refused and hoped I'd heard the last
of it when she sulkily retired to her room.

Hours later she wakened me. 'Those horse-thieves are
in the kitchen,' she gasped in an agonized whisper. 'I've
been listening to them several minutes. They're trying
not to make a noise, but they've been in the pantry. I heard
them take the lid off the roaster!'

I sat up hurriedly. 'You're imagining things,' I said, but I said it in a low voice. I wanted to believe that she was exaggerating as usual, but a shiver ran up and down my spine.

'I knew you wouldn't believe me,' she sniveled. 'Come and listen for yourself.'

I tiptoed to her room, which was over the kitchen, and listened tensely. She had told the truth. Someone was in the pantry... I too heard muffled, cautious sounds... We crept back to my room and consulted in a frozen panic.

There was only one room in the house that possessed a key, and this was the bathroom. The cook had long bemoaned this shocking lack of caution on our part, and now she insisted that we wake the children and lock ourselves into the bathroom until the danger was past. I've always hated locked places, and the idea of being shut into one small room with a couple of desperate men loose in the house was more than I could contemplate.

'No,' I whispered sternly. 'We've got to go to the bunkhouse for help.'

Her eyes bulged with horror and suddenly she began to cry, '*I'm scared to go down those steps.*'

We were wasting time and I had reached the limit of my patience. 'All right, then. You stay here with the children. I'll go.'

But that she wouldn't hear to. She refused to be left, and it was decided that we should waken the children and make our escape together. It seemed foolhardy to start down those stairs with no means of protecting ourselves, and I could think of no suitable weapon. I remembered suddenly a story I had once read about a bandit who held up a stagecoach with a pair of scissors. Secretly, because the children had been awakened by this time and I did not want to

emphasize the need for defense, I armed myself with a pair
of shears and headed the procession that crept down the
stairs. I still remember the comfort the cold steel of those
scissors gave to my clammy, even colder hand.

We had almost reached the front door when Wezie
stumbled and started to cry. For one ghastly moment we
all stood still, paralyzed with fright.... There was the
shattering sound of an overturned chair from the kitchen.
I grabbed Wezie up in my arms and we fell over each other
as we leaped through the door.... A screen slammed, and
then we really put on some speed, shrieking at the top of our
lungs as we ran. Wezie was five years old and so awkward
to carry that I couldn't keep up with the rest; they had
reached the gate — were leaving me behind. As I rounded
the side of the house in a panic, I collided with a man! My
knees collapsed and I slumped to the ground.

'What's wrong!'

Even then I couldn't believe it was Tom! When he tried
to take our howling daughter from my arms, I clung to her
as though he was the desperado I had believed him to be.
He had been in the kitchen all the time; had concluded his
business much sooner than he'd hoped, had not stopped to
eat dinner on the way home, and had been preparing himself
a meal as quietly as possible so as not to arouse the household.

When we had collected the children and the cook and
reassured the men from the bunkhouse, who by now were
tearing across the creek, jerking on trousers and shirts as
they came, I remembered my scissors. I hadn't the vaguest
notion where I'd lost them. I had not mentioned my bright
idea when I related the story of our attempted escape to
Tom. I'd forgotten all about it, and now it did not seem
like such a bright idea. I decided the shears were somewhere
in the grass and I'd wait until morning to find them.

I stepped on them as we came through the front door and recovered them surreptitiously. Whatever claims I may have had to daring died, in that moment, an ignoble death. And the sight of a pair of shears still has the power to take a tuck in my ego.

The sheriff's method of tracking the thieves was effective, though. Two spent and saddle-galled horses were picked up in the hills seven miles from our ranch the next day and the thieves were eventually arrested, on foot, not many miles distant.

I7

Calamities

OUR neighbor, Mr. Thayer, does not have Forest allotments for all of his sheep, and one band runs on his ranch the year round. Several days ago a part of this band had a pile-up and thirty ewes died of suffocation. I learned this via the country telephone line but I tuned in too late to get all the details. I'm sorry I missed the first of the conversation. Mr. Thayer was wrathy. He was talking to the county attorney and his concluding remarks had all the explosive emphasis of a string of firecrackers. I gathered that his sheep had piled up in a newly dug prospect hole.

'I ain't got enough holes and gullies on this ranch,' he shouted, the wires vibrating with the depths of his emotion, 'I ain't got enough, so all the prospectors in the county are helping me out by digging some more.'

The county attorney tried to say something about trespass signs but Mr. Thayer cut him short. 'Trespass signs!' he bellowed. 'What good's a trespass sign when the Government's howling for manganese and tungsten? I lost thirty ewes in a prospect hole! What I want to know — *is* this my ranch, or *ain't* it? Is there any law in the county seat to protect me from pests, or have I got to protect myself?'

The county attorney announced hastily that he would drive right over and Mr. Thayer hung up.

I smiled as I put the receiver back on its hook. I could understand Mr. Thayer's indignation. Since the defense program got under way we've had a lot of trouble with overzealous prospectors. There is some manganese and tungsten in this vicinity; high-grade ore, but in such small quantities that it would hardly pay to work it. Years ago we looked into the possibility of development and discarded any notions we had of wresting a fortune from the land. The itinerant prospector is not so easily discouraged. He roams the hills, comes on a pocket of manganese or tungsten, and the bubble of his enthusiasm seldom bursts before he has dug a number of pitfalls for sheep. What he hopes to gain should he uncover something of value on another man's land is a mystery, but he persists just the same. Mr. Thayer was right. We already have enough gullies and holes for sheep to pile up in. We don't need the prospector's help.

A pile-up is the most dreaded of all calamities in the sheep country, and it strikes with the speed and fatality of a bolt of lightning at any season of the year. The lead sheep will stumble or come headlong against some obstruction which cannot be got over quickly — a cliff of rocks, a steep hollow or a fence. The oncoming herd, unable to stop because of pressure from behind, climb up and up, trampling the first layer of sheep to the ground — the next layer and the next, until there is a writhing mountain of wool.

Sometimes as many as three to five hundred sheep perish from suffocation in a few moments. If the herder is on hand, half the sheep involved may be saved. But even then the herder must use his head. The dogs are no help in this type of emergency. Their barking only increases the general confusion and terror. What sheep survive must be dragged off bodily, so the outcome of a pile-up depends wholly upon the speed and dexterity of the herder.

Should strayed sheep pile up, less than ten per cent may come out alive. One winter I saw the result of a strayed-sheep pile-up in a little coulee which was approximately ten feet wide and ten feet deep. It was filled to the level of the surrounding country with dead sheep and the few survivors were calmly grazing on the far side, having gained this sanctuary by using the backs of their less fortunate sisters for a bridge.

Ordinarily the dead can be pelted and a portion of the loss retrieved, but I remember one pile-up that happened seven years ago on this ranch when we were unable to recover even the pelts of the sheep which had perished. We lost three hundred ewes and that pile-up made history in the Valley. The only thing we ever got out of it was the doubtful satisfaction of being able always to tell a better pile-up story than the other fellow — with no fear of contradiction.

This pile-up took place in February, the coldest month in Montana. One of our herders and his sheep were camped near the Madison River. The thermometer had been hovering between thirty-five and forty below zero for a week, and for hours on end a furious wind had been blowing. The wind died down at dusk on the night of the big pile-up, but the cold remained. The herder bedded his sheep near the wagon, prepared a meal for himself and his dogs and retired early. Shortly after he got himself comfortably settled in his bunk, the dogs began to whine with the still, deadly cold — to leap and scratch against the door. The man took pity on the animals, got up and let them into the wagon, first making sure that the sheep were safe on the bed-ground.

During the night the wind sprang up again, and it began to snow. The herder was so fatigued from his day of exposure that he slept through these signals of danger. Now, there's nothing in the world that will cause sheep to become so restless as a high, cold wind. The wind penetrates their fleece, they endure the cold and discomfort just so long and then they begin thinking about seeking better shelter. When the dogs are on guard their restlessness gets no further than thinking, for the dogs start to bark at the first move and warn the herder.

Sometime in the middle of that fatal night the sheep left the bed-ground. They traveled with the wind and somewhere along the way the band split. One bunch went into the foothills and were later recovered with only a small loss. The other bunch followed the course of the river for several miles and came presently to a place where the river made a decided bend, almost a horseshoe bend. The land was low here and a side hill gave the sheep the protection they had been seeking, so they bedded down again.

Before morning the river gorged and cut a new channel straight across the bend, leaving the sheep marooned on what was now a small island between the new channel and the original one.

I've been told that there is only one other river in the world which has the peculiarities of the Madison River. Other rivers freeze from the top down, but the Madison freezes from the bottom up. The bed of the river is covered with great boulders. Slush ice forms on top, sinks and clings to these boulders, and little by little the ice builds up until the river gorges. The water backs up then and floods all the surrounding country.

When our sheep were first trapped in the bend there were around one hundred acres of dry ground on the small island. As the river continued to back up this ground became flooded. At first the sheep huddled together, but as the water rose and there was no longer enough dry ground for all to have a footing, they were terrified, lost their heads and began to climb on one another's backs.

The bottom layer of sheep perished and as the water grew deeper the others kept scrambling upward, the stronger trampling the weaker beneath their hoofs, until several layers of sheep lay dead. The survivors, those on top, just managed to keep their heads above water. As the night wore on the water in this newly flooded area, which was practically free of rocks, began to freeze in normal fashion, from top to bottom, and the upper portions of the sheep's bodies were locked tight in ice.

Toward dawn, when the herder got up to turn his dogs out, he discovered that all of his sheep were missing. He hurried into his clothes and set out to look for them. But he was at a loss to know which way they had gone. The wind, which could have determined the general direction, at least, had stopped blowing and all tracks of the strays had been obliterated by the falling snow.

The distracted herder hunted for hours before he located his sheep, and then he was too shocked to believe his eyes. He looked out on what appeared to be a solid lake of ice, into which several hundred live sheep were frozen to the neck. It was a sight that might have dazed a more imaginative brain than his. I saw this phenomena several hours later and I know just how he felt. I shall never forget that expanse of rigid, bodiless heads, the wild, staring eyes or the feeble blats that came from too few exhausted throats.

The situation was one the herder could not hope to cope with alone. It was foreign to anything he had ever experienced and he set out immediately for help. He was ten miles from the home ranch but less than five from the county road, which he reached in a couple of arduous hours. He was lucky enough to encounter a rancher who was hauling hay. The rancher got to a telephone as quickly as possible and relayed his message.

We had reason to thank the country telephone that day. When we arrived at the river with a truckload of men — armed with shovels, sheep crooks and pickaxes — we found a number of our neighbors had got there before us. The rancher who lived nearest had driven down to the river, looked the situation over and rushed back to his ranch for a number of lambing panels and some lengths of rope. These panels were tied together and made into rafts, upon which the sheep were lifted as fast as they could be chopped out of the ice.

The rescue of those ice-bound ewes is something nobody present will ever forget. It began in early afternoon and it was completed by lantern light around ten o'clock that night. As the day wore on the storm increased in velocity. The driving, swirling snow beat against the faces of the rescue party, all but blinding them.

The rafts had to be dragged out to the sheep by hand (and when darkness came, on hands and knees). It was a tricky and dangerous procedure. The ice in the bend had frozen less than a foot from the top. Beneath this ice there was seven or more feet of treacherous, rushing water. One false step or careless shifting of weight could easily break this ice and plunge a man to his death before help could reach him. In spite of precautions two men did break through to their waists, but they managed to scramble out and worked along with the rest in stiff, frozen clothing until every last sheep was hauled to high, dry land.

Those ewes were the strangest sight I have ever seen. They could scarcely walk because chunks of ice weighing easily twenty-five pounds still clung to their backs and bodies, and they were forced to carry this fantastic burden about for weeks before it finally melted and came loose from their wool. The unbelievable part of this pile-up is that not one sheep rescued was any the worse for her experience. But the pile-up cost us dearly, nevertheless, because the dead sheep were locked tight in the gorge and when the ice broke in the spring the pelts were worthless.

A pile-up heads the list of sheep calamities, but strayed sheep can get into more trouble than it's possible to foresee or guard against. I never think of the lines of the nursery rhyme,

> *Leave them alone and they'll come home*
> *Wagging their tails behind them,*

without smiling. Lost sheep seldom come home, and if they should it's an accident. You go after them. You go after them in winter, sometimes in the face of a howling blizzard. You flounder through snowdrifts, on horseback and on foot. You freeze your hands and feet, but you dare not turn back. Each hour's delay decreases your chance of finding the strays alive. It's a ten-to-one bet that the coyotes, in any case, will prove better hunters than you, or the strays will meet disaster in a pile-up.

You go after them in spring and summer too. The coyotes are still on the prowl and there is another menace that

can prove just as fatal: the noxious weed. The woolgrower
has never been able to stamp out such weeds as death camas,
lupine, larkspur, and loco weed from his range. They spring
up in a different place every year, and he can only put his
faith in his herder's ability to recognize the weeds a jump
ahead of the sheep and herd them in the opposite direction.
Death camas and lupine will poison and kill. Larkspur seldom affects the ewes but it is fatal to young lambs.

And lupine . . . It's still hard for me to believe that a blossom so lovely as the lupine could be a deadly poison. I've
always had a secret affection for this weed because it so
closely resembles the bluebonnet, the state flower of Texas.
'Resembles, my eye!' says Tom. 'Bluebonnets are lupine
and you know it. The Ranger told you so.' For many years
we've argued this question heatedly.

Many times I've regretted the sentimental enthusiasm
which led me, years ago, to boast of the lovely blue fields of
Texas. More times I've regretted the thoughtfulness of a
young cousin who sent me a large box of bluebonnets the
second spring I lived here. They arrived in fair shape and
Tom came into the kitchen as I was arranging them in a
vase.

'My God!' he exclaimed. 'Where did you get that
lupine?' He wasn't joking; he was really concerned.

When I corrected him in an injured voice, he shouted
with laughter. My bluebonnets, he told me, were nothing
but lupine, poison weeds that were fatal to grazing sheep.
Were there so few wild flowers in Texas that we had to
choose a noxious weed for an emblem? He warned me not
to throw them outdoors when they withered; to burn every
last one of them, so their seeds wouldn't scatter.

The loco weed drives sheep crazy. Once they get a taste

of it, the habit is acquired and a ewe will trace it down from season to season with the zeal and stealth of a drug addict who has been without dope for days. It has the most astonishing effect on her. She will leap into the air, back up suddenly and begin to race round and round in a circle. Unless she is captured and hobbled she will continue to run in circles until she dies from exhaustion. You can imagine a herder's dilemma should he find himself with a hundred or more locoed ewes on his hands.

Death camas is fatal. One spring we lost seventy-six sheep which had strayed onto a hillside where this weed grew. One of my brothers was in Montana at the time and when Tom took several men out to pelt the dead, my brother and I went along. The carcasses of those sheep were strewn over acres of ground. My brother helped drag them all to a central spot and then he crawled into the car with me to watch the pelting.

'I'm disillusioned,' he teased. 'You told me sheep were smart.'

'They are smart.'

He grinned. 'I suppose this was a suicide pact? Just seventy-six ewes which got ta'red of it all?'

'Baloney,' I said; 'you're allergic to fish, but I notice *you* eat it.'

It has always seemed to me that a sheep has enough to contend with, just being a sheep. It doesn't seem fair that she should also be the helpless target of insects and birds and beasts. So many foes prey upon her that it would be hard to decide which is worst. Blowflies probably.

No matter how careful a shearer may be, he will nick a sheep somewhere before he has finished shearing her. The larger cuts are seldom overlooked, but should a small cut escape the notice of the brander, the sheep's life is endangered. Blowflies are always thickest at the shearing pens. They buzz around the sheep and lay eggs in any undoctored wounds. Maggots hatch and these eat into the ewe's flesh. Eventually she becomes crazed with pain, wanders off and often dies before she is found.

The sheep tick is another insect that torments a ewe and there is absolutely no way of combating ticks. They imbed themselves in the helpless ewe's flesh, and the frantic creature rolls on the ground in an effort to be rid of them.

A ewe is so constructed that it is almost impossible for her to turn over once she gets on her back. Her wool flattens out, her stomach distends, and it makes no difference how wildly she struggles, she cannot right herself without help. If she has been on green pasture a gas forms, crowds her heart, and she will die in an incredibly short time unless she is set on her feet. This danger is especially prevalent during the lambing season when the ewe's body is clumsy and heavy with lamb.

Sheep dip may discourage a blowfly, but it doesn't bother the magpie. These pests are always in evidence. If there's a cut on the sheep's back, the magpie moves in. And when I say moves in, I mean exactly that, for magpies will light on a defenseless ewe's back and ride for hours on end, pecking at open wounds as they ride. If the distracted ewe rolls on her back and by some miracle of equilibrium can right herself again, she has gained nothing but a few moments' respite. The magpie is still hovering about, scolding, chattering with impatience to resume the interrupted meal.

Lambs are also the constant prey of magpies, which follow the drop band with the noisy insistence of gulls in the wake of a ship. Sometimes the sky is thick with them. They are not content to feast upon the ever-present carcasses; their favorite pastime is the blinding of baby lambs.

Young lambs have a habit of straying from the herd, locating a sunny sheltered spot and dropping off to sleep. The magpies are always alert and the moment they spy a lone sleeping lamb, they pounce down and peck out its eyes.

Magpies are as bold as swashbuckling pirates and the presence of a lamber gives them little concern. They are clever too. They seem to know that a lamber is far too busy to spend time picking them off one by one with his gun. If it were not for the dogs, which are sent ever so often to round up the strays, the magpies could do an unbelievable amount of damage to the lamb crop.

One year after the magpies had blinded an alarming number of our lambs, somebody told Tom that a huge chunk of beef, soaked in arsenic and hung in a tree, would take care of the marauders for all time. His adviser claimed to have tried it out successfully. The magpies were supposed to quit that vicinity permanently so soon as they discovered a shocking decrease in their flock. At his wit's end, Tom was in a mood to experiment with anything. He poisoned a chunk of beef and took it to one of the drop bands.

When he returned that night I met him at the gate. 'Did it work?' I wanted to know.

'I'll say it worked,' he replied ruefully. 'It worked so well for the magpies that we had to move the drop band better than a mile. For every magpie that was poisoned, ten more swarmed in!'

The coyote is the traditional enemy of sheep and an ever-present one, but he seldom molests a ewe if there is lamb to be had. The coyote has wearied of an exclusive diet of mutton during the long winter months and in the spring he stalks the lambs, watching his chance for a kill. The wool-growers of this country have done everything possible to combat the inroads of the coyote, but they still lose far too large a percentage of their lamb crop to this beast. The lambers and herders manage to handle the situation in the daytime, but it is under cover of night that the coyote works best.

During lambing our hills are dotted with small bunches of ewes (fifty or more in a bunch) whose lambs are approximately the same age. Until there are enough of these small bunches to form a herd and require a herder, they are put out to graze near the various camps. The coyotes always hover about and if something were not done to frighten them away, they would soon kill off the lambs.

There are two methods of protecting the lambs, and the more popular one is known as 'flagging.' A lighted lantern is placed inside a small canvas tepee which has been set up near each bunch of ewes and lambs. The coyote has a wholesome respect for Man, and a light to him denotes Man's proximity. Only the direst pangs of hunger will cause the coyote to ignore this danger signal.

Another method which we have found to be fairly effective is the use of the sulphur smudge. This smudge is placed all over the lambing range and it throws out a horrible odor. The smell is very distasteful to the coyote, and he usually gives the vicinity a wide berth. Unfortunately this latter method is an expensive one, and it also entails an almost prohibitive amount of time and work.

I have about decided that the coyote will always be a problem, and the best thing we can do for our own peace of mind is to charge his inroads off to normal loss. If the time ever comes when the sheepmen of Montana can do this cheerfully, they will be spared a lot of futile worry.

Coyotes are exceptionally thick in this part of the Valley. Only last winter a native trapper got fifty full-grown coyotes on our ranch alone, and this spring he had sixty-five cubs to his credit.

Trappers have various methods of trapping coyotes. The most effective is the use of poisoned bait. The carcass of a cow or horse is treated with a mixture of arsenic and strychnine and placed in a likely spot. Sometimes a dozen or more coyotes will be poisoned before the beasts decide that the neighborhood is not a healthy spot.

But poison bait has not found favor with the sheepman, since it can prove just as fatal to his dogs. We lost so many sheep dogs from poison that Tom has not permitted its use on his range for a good many years. He's reached the conclusion that coyotes can be thinned out best through the destruction of the pups before they are old enough to leave the den.

Most trappers in this country have an amazing knowledge of wood and trail lore, which is invaluable to them in detecting a coyote den. They have several unique methods of securing the pups. Some trappers drag them out with a length of barbed wire which has been doubled and twisted so that one end forms a loop which will not slip from the hand. The opposite end is bent into two prongs. These are poked around in a den until contact is made with a pup. As soon as the prongs have become fast in the squirming pup's fur, he can be dragged forth with a minimum of trouble.

Other trappers use small, game dogs for their work. The dog squeezes his way through the tunnel into the den and brings the pups back one by one. It isn't so simple as it sounds if the coyote bitch should chance to be at home. It's a battle to the death then, and the best dog wins. I've had several trappers tell me of the moments of suspense and anxiety they experience standing helplessly on the outside of a den, with the muffled sounds of battle in their ears. And when at last there comes a silence, the suspense is even greater, for the trapper can never be sure whether a friendly little black-and-white dog or a snarling coyote bitch will presently leap out of the mouth of the tunnel.

The black bear seldom molest our sheep or destroy our camps on the ranch, where the herder lives in a wagon, but they are an ever increasing nuisance on the Forest Reserve. Here, because of government regulations, the herder's shelter is a tent. Our Forest, known as the Beaverhead Forest, skirts the Yellowstone Park and it is literally infested with bear; especially so since a recent Park ruling has prohibited the feeding of bear by tourists.

Many of these Park bear, unable to secure the sweets they crave, have wandered into the Forest Reserve. Here they make nocturnal raids on the sheep and demolish many camps. Nothing is safe from them. Each year they take their toll of our ewes and lambs, and wreck countless camps.

Not content with gorging themselves upon all the bacon, ham, lard, sugar and jam they can get their paws upon, they destroy everything in sight. They rip open sacks of flour, force the lids from baking powder and coffee tins and strew the contents on the ground. They overturn the stoves and claw the tent and the herder's clothes and bed to ribbons.

The herder has no way of protecting himself against this vandalism because Forest regulations protect the bear. A herder is not permitted to kill unless he catches a bear in the act of destroying sheep or razing a camp. Unfortunately, bears raid the sheep at night and destroy property during the day while the herder is out with his sheep, making it next to impossible to identify the marauder.

I recall one herder of ours who had his camp clawed to ribbons three times in one summer. Shortly after the bear's third raid Tom and I made a special trip into the Forest to

console him. We found him sitting dejectedly on a big rock
with his head in his hands. His overalls were sewed up from
stem to stern with white binding twine and his shirt was in
tatters — quite beyond mending. He looked exactly like
a scarecrow.

'Had a little accident?' Tom asked, trying to suppress
his mirth.

The herder raised his head and scowled. 'Yep,' he
brought out grimly, 'and it's the kind of accident that's
stopped being healthy.' A sickly grin spread over his face.
'You know — I've been sort of envying my sheep. A bear
can't skin them but once.'

Thereupon he began to tell us his troubles. When he finished the story he said: 'The worst of it is, I know which
bear done it. I've seen the old she-devil lurking about in
the trees. I've laid for her time and again, but she's too
slick. I've never been able to catch her doing me dirt. But
I know she done it and the next time I lay eyes on her, she's
going to get it in the head.'

'No,' Tom warned, 'you can't do that. I don't want any
trouble with the Rangers. You've just got to keep your eyes
open and catch her in the act.'

But the herder did not heed his warning, for the next
week Tom got an urgent call requesting him to report to
the Forest Ranger Station. The Ranger informed him that
he'd got word, by mountain grapevine, that one of our
herders had shot and killed a bear which was not molesting
him.

Together they drove up to interview the man, who
launched immediately into the story he had told Tom and
me the week before.

'Now, that's too bad and I'm sorry about it,' the Ranger
said. 'You're within your rights if you catch a bear de-

stroying sheep or property. But you killed this bear when she wasn't anywhere near your camp or sheep.'

The herder's silence convicted him and his complacent look angered the Ranger, who demanded sternly: 'How do you know the bear you killed was a stock-destroying bear? You didn't catch her in the act.'

The herder grinned now and scratched his head. 'Well,' he drawled, 'I don't exactly know it, but I know this much: she ain't a stock-destroying bear any more!'

18

The depression hits us

THERE was a decade in my life here which passed with incredible swiftness. From 1921 to 1931 I was too busy keeping up with my children to find time for outside activities of any kind, to give much thought to the mechanics of the ranch. It was in these years, however, that I definitely put down roots and thought of myself as a Montanan.

They were largely good years. The children grew like healthy young animals. They ate and slept and played and rode horseback, and they were happy and content. They wanted nothing more. As a matter of fact they begrudged every day spent away from the ranch. In 1928 I took them to Texas. That visit was a nightmare. I'm sure my family were heartily glad to have us say good-bye. I know I was glad to say it.

My children, I found, were misfits, were not remotely interested in the things that amused and delighted their young cousins and, with a frankness that put me to shame, they never failed to mention it. I was cross with them and they with me, and their seeming rudeness shocked and alarmed my people.

For one thing, their young cousins said, 'Yes, ma'am' and 'No, sir.' Leigh, Andy, and Wezie said 'Yes' and 'No' flatly. For years I had tried to get the 'ma'am' and 'sir' angle across without success. Nor had I been able to sell them the Montana substitute of 'Yes, Mother,' and 'No, Dad.' I always meant to do something about it, but I waited too long.

At the ranch I had actually thought of them as fairly good children. They were full of life and a little too adventurous for comfort, but they seldom got out of hand. In the soft-speaking background of Texas I discovered, to my dismay and chagrin, that I'd been raising a trio of young savages.

They missed the ranch, its space and freedom. The restrictions of a city smothered every good instinct and trait they possessed. As soon as the newness wore off they wanted to go home. They ganged up on me, and the time I planned to spend with my old friends was spent riding herd on three outlaws, whom I was ashamed to claim for my own, whitewashing their rudeness and apologizing for their lack of appreciation.

When I overheard one sister tell another that our mother would turn in her grave if she could see how I was rearing my children, I decided it was time to take drastic measures. Not ten minutes later Andy blacked the eye of a young cousin who put up a spirited defense of his bicycle, in a bicycle-versus-horse argument. I made the mistake of demanding that Andy apologize to his victim and he promptly refused. I marched him into my bedroom and shut the door.

'I don't know what's got into you,' I stormed. 'John had as much right to defend his bicycle as you had to defend your pony. You're downright mean.'

'I feel mean,' my son admitted sulkily. 'I don't like it here. There's nothing to do.'

Nothing to do . . . Trips to the zoo, swimming parties in a lovely tiled pool . . . and picnics. It had seemed a lot to me when I was small, but as I gazed at my son's flushed, sulky face and turned the matter over in my mind, I suddenly got his slant and a wave of nostalgia swept over me.

A trip to the zoo . . . animals pacing restlessly back and forth behind bars or lying inert on the sawdust floors of their cages . . . blank, lack-luster eyes staring indifferently into space. All right for a city child who has no chance to see wild life in the open. But not for a boy who has looked out his window and glimpsed deer and antelope and elk grazing contentedly on the hills. Not for a boy who has made a supreme sacrifice so that a creature he loved might be free.

I thought of the Andy who had raised Speckles, a wounded fawn, to maturity and then turned her loose in the mountains; the small boy I had found face down in the grass sobbing his heart out because Speckles was gone.

'Darling — if you care so terribly,' I remembered asking, 'why did you let her go?'

And I could still see a pair of tightly clenched fists and the set little mouth which had told me bleakly: 'She had to be *free*. Don't you see, Mother? Speckles had to be free.'

A tidy swimming pool . . . bathing suits. For children accustomed to swimming in high mountain lakes . . . naked bronze bodies flashing in and out of water so clear it reflected every cloud in the sky.

Picnics ... in groves with stoves and tables and benches ... against the piercing sweet smoke of a spruce-log camp-fire ... tin plates balanced carelessly on sturdy brown knees ... No, it wasn't good enough.

I had brought Andy into that room to thrash him soundly. Instead I fought back tears and hugged his strong little shoulders. I was homesick too. ... We had a heart-to-heart talk and when we were through I called Wezie and Leigh and made a bargain. If they'd behave for just one week, we'd go home. They did and we did.

The boys came of school age at the peak of a cycle of prosperity in Montana. The question of transportation to the country school five miles from the ranch reared its head and we decided to engage a tutor and start them out at home. We built a log cabin and fitted it up for a school-room. The arrangement proved satisfactory. In 1931 we began to feel the pinch of the depression which resulted from the débâcle of 1929 and could no longer afford the expense of a tutor. We then enrolled the children in the district school and until the weather became too bad I drove them back and forth.

Before the first winter was over I began to wonder if the end was worth the struggle and to wish that our youngsters could follow the example of some poor whites, sharecropping on my grandfather's Texas farm, who, to use the words of my negro nurse when she warned me sternly to stay away from them, had 'jes' sort of run around and growed.'

Recently a college professor said to me: 'I like to teach boys and girls who have been raised on ranches. They're good students and make high grades. I've found the average student values a college education in direct proportion to the difficulty he's had arriving that far.'

The difficulty *he's* had! I opened my mouth to protest and closed it firmly again. The college professor was young and profoundly interested in his work. I could not bear to disillusion him by announcing that fifty per cent of the ranch boys and girls of my acquaintance (my own included) would never have got past the fourth grade of school without prodding from their parents.

They've had difficulty, there's no denying that, but they've had fun as well; and it hasn't been fun for their parents. For every child who has completed grade school from an isolated ranch, there are parents who have gone to school three times over — in toil, in patience and in perseverance!

I can still see Tom, on a sub-zero morning, bending over the engine of our car with a blowtorch in his hand trying to thaw out the motor. I remember the relief on his face when, sometimes an hour later, he got the first stuttering response to his efforts.

I have known ranchers who, in winter, got up morning after morning to milk cows and feed stock before dawn, so that time could be found to drive their children to school; who often performed these same tasks at night when the drifted roads delayed them after school. Most ranch men in this country have more work than they can accomplish under normal conditions. If they're willing to sacrifice several hours a day, five days a week, to the cause of education, they deserve some credit too.

The rancher with a large family to put through school has my deepest sympathy and understanding. Too well I know what he's up against. I've taken my daily dozen at the business end of a shovel more times than I can count. You've no idea how this form of exercise can dim your enthusiasm for, and undermine the importance of, education. Looking back, I'm sure our children owe their early education to the fact that they too were ready and eager to quit any time Tom or I said the word. I shall never forget the day I first discovered this.

It was bitterly cold and a high wind was blowing. Ordinarily I should not have attempted the trip on such a day, but that morning Tom and all the men on the ranch had set out to look for lost sheep. If the children got to school, I had to take them.

We had gone scarcely a mile when our car skidded out of the track and landed in a snowbank. My two sons and I took turns at the shovel until we were short of temper, red of face and panting with exhaustion, and still the car wouldn't budge. When my turn came for the third time I thrust the shovel savagely against the under side of the running-board and in doing so ripped a fingernail off to the quick.

'Oh, what's the use,' I wailed, sucking my injured finger, 'what's the use of school?'

Just then I caught sight of Andy's face. His eyes were dancing with excitement and he wore a grin tucked in from ear to ear.

'Do you really mean it, Mother?' he demanded jubilantly. 'Could we quit today?' He caught my arm and sought to persuade me. 'We know enough. We can figure a shearer's tally and count the pounds of wool in a clip. That's all we need to know.'

That's all we need to know! In no surer way could he have put starch in my weary backbone. I started to shovel again.

We did not feel the full weight of the last depression until the summer of 1931. We'd been cutting corners, expecting it, but even so we were wholly unprepared for the tragic four years that followed. I had thought I knew something about depressions. I found I didn't.

Many things contributed to making these years the blackest in the history of the livestock industry in Montana. Nature played a leading rôle; for three years drought took over the land. The grass on our range burned up before it fairly started to grow. Streams dried up and the melting snow in the mountains was sucked into the parched earth before it could reach the irrigation ditches. Our hay crops, for lack of proper irrigation, were less than fifty per cent of normal. On top of this a plague of grasshoppers devoured four sections of grazing at Stonyacres; they cleaned acres of land all over the state.

We went into the winter of 1931–32 with insufficient grazing and feed. Remembering the bitter experience of 1919–20 we shipped in large quantities of cottonseed cake and corn to supplement the hay. As it turned out we were lucky, since we had no trouble financing this additional expense. Our credit was still good, and we had the old-time country banker behind us.

The old-time country banker was the stockman's best friend. He was wise and just and he knew all his borrowers personally. He was familiar with their problems, their outfits and their methods of operation and his loans were based largely on moral risks. He trusted the judgment of the men he financed year after year; was confident of their ability to secure the highest possible price for the commodities they had to sell. He advised, when his advice was solicited, but he seldom interfered.

The old-time banker had been hard pressed to take care of his customers in 1931 but he had done it. In normal or somewhat less than normal years the woolgrower could have paid off a large percentage of his notes after his wool was sold and his lambs shipped. But now the price of lambs and wool took a terrific slump and the value of breeding ewes decreased accordingly. A man who had borrowed fifty or sixty per cent of the value of his flock found he owed better than one hundred per cent.

Then came the bank holiday and the exit of the old-time banker from the picture. The banks opened under government regulations which — rightly, I'm sure — placed rigid restrictions on all loans. The new set-up required liquid assets for collateral, which the woolgrower no longer had. His land could not be moved at any price and his sheep were mortgaged beyond their current market value. Every woolgrower in the valley faced bankruptcy.

In order to place the banks again on sound footing, many loans had to be written off for whatever could be salvaged, which resulted in loss and consequent drastic reduction of the capital stocks of most of the banks. No bank could lend more than twenty per cent of its capital stock to any one customer, and in our case, and in the case of many other stockmen, this wasn't enough. There was an appalling discrepancy between the amount that could be borrowed and the amount needed properly to finance a stockman's operations. It costs just as much or more to run sheep in lean years as in good ones. Retrenchment may be possible in ranch operation, in upkeep and in personal sacrifice, but the sheep have to be cared for and fed regardless.

With lack of adequate financing the woolgrower literally had his back to the wall. It was a daily humiliating struggle to keep things together and many sheepmen were wiped out.

To take care of this unprecedented emergency the Government stepped in and the Regional Agricultural Credit Corporation came into being. The struggling banks reluctantly waived their first mortgages and the RACC took over.

The confusion and tragedy that followed this switch was appalling. Because of red tape and lack of understanding it was no longer possible for a livestock man to telephone his banker in the midst of an unexpected blizzard, request additional funds for feed and receive them promptly. He was forced to go through a harrowing exchange of letters, telephone calls and telegrams before the wheels could be set rolling, and the emergency might have passed and a heavy loss resulted before help could be got. Blizzards don't wait on red tape.

Furthermore, in order to fit the topheavy loans into regulations of the RACC the woolgrower was compelled to reduce his flock. In the past he had made up normal loss by holding back the best of his ewe lambs when he shipped. Now he was compelled to sell his entire lamb crop for several years.

All this was hard enough, but the bitterest pill the woolgrower had to swallow was government supervision from a swivel chair. The sheepman could no longer use his own judgment in marketing his crops. He was told when to hold and when to sell — and at what price — by, in most cases, men who had no knowledge of the conditions and weather under which he had to operate.[1]

The woolgrowers came out of that depression heavily in debt, with greatly reduced flocks which it would take years

[1] In all justice I must say that the tragic situation which existed before the Production Credit Associations (another branch of government financing) were organized was due largely to lack of knowledge and understanding on the part of the management of the RACC. This mistake was recognized and rectified when the PCA's took over the RACC loans. Borrowers were permitted to elect their own managers and they elected men who were familiar with livestock and the conditions under which they were run. Their managers, so far as government regulations will permit, follow in the footsteps of the old-time banker. They have set up funds to take care of emergencies; they allow their borrowers, in most cases, to market their crops when, and at any price, they deem best, and they are cooperative in every possible way.

to build back to normal again. Those were years I'd like to forget, but just the same it was then that I learned the meaning of courage and sacrifice and indomitable faith in a business. I saw Tom's hair turn gray and lines of worry etched into his face, but never once did he speak, or even think, of giving up.

I'm not proud of the part I played. There came a time when I could see no ray of hope ahead; a time when I was more than anxious to give up; a time when I pleaded with Tom to salvage what he could while there was a chance to save something — and clear out. I reminded him that our children had to be educated, that they trusted us and we had no right to betray that trust.

Education — as I saw it slipping away — became tremendously important. I tortured myself with visions of the children growing up without advantages — ill-equipped to meet the problems of life. I spoke of it only once. I wanted to, time and again, but I couldn't forget the look on Tom's face, the incredulity, the hurt and disappointment. Sheep would come back, he told me briefly; they always had.

'But suppose they don't?' I cried out desperately. 'All signs fail sometime... For you and me — yes; but we've got to think about the children.'

'The children will have to take their chance along with the rest of us,' he replied. 'It isn't going to hurt them.'

How right he was! Those years made men of our boys, laid the groundwork for the stability and tenacity of purpose which has characterized their endeavors ever since. Without any prompting Leigh and Andy pitched in and helped with the ranch work as they had never helped before. They were only boys but they did the work of men. They learned the value of money, to count it in so many hours of toil.

But they learned something else: they learned that they did not want to follow in Tom's footsteps and become sheepmen. They loved every inch of the ranch, they liked farming and haying, but they did not like sheep. They had not inherited the traditional patience which is as much a part of the successful sheepman as the air he breathes.

I remember a day when Tom sent them out to catch an old ewe which had been left behind by the herd. They'd been told many times that they could never catch a ewe by dashing up to her, but they always did. The old ewe eluded them, refused to be caught and led them a merry chase for more than an hour. She wasn't caught until she collapsed with exhaustion. When the boys had corralled her they dragged themselves into the house. Their faces were begrimed with dirt and their clothes all but torn off them.

'*Mother!*' Andy panted. '*Remember this: I'll never be a sheepman.*'

Leigh collapsed into a chair and eyed him scornfully. 'Are you just now finding that out? I decided I wouldn't two years ago.' And that day, as young as they were, I began to face the fact that Tom might have to carry on alone.

19

Dudes

Tom and I disagree about many things. We are as different in taste and disposition as any two people could possibly be. But we enjoy our differences of opinion and are amazed and a little resentful when we occasionally find our views in perfect accord.

All I have ever needed to whet my lagging interest in a subject has been a thumb's-down gesture from Tom. His disapproval has an amazing effect upon me. My brain is swept clean of all vagueness and doubt. My convictions take shape with sudden clarity, and argument only makes me doubly sure that I'm right. I sometimes give in, just to prove that I'm a good sport, but I often wonder regretfully how a situation might have worked out if I'd listened to **my** hunch instead of Tom's.

One thing we've never seen eye to eye is the dude. In summer there are more dudes than natives in this Valley. We have three big commercial dude ranches, and some of the oldest and best cattle outfits have been bought up and are being operated by Eastern dudes who live here the year around.

These dudes raise stock the same as we. I consider them natives in everything but name. Tom claims they aren't. He says they do not operate under the same conditions; that when a bad year comes they need only reach into another pocket, make up their losses and run their spreads as usual. We have to take what comes on the chin and work our way to normal, which, according to Tom, is quite another thing.

Nevertheless, the dudes interest me enormously. I like them. They are a social, friendly people and can be found at the postoffice in the small town nearest our ranch almost any afternoon.

Until my children went off to school and later settled and married in other states, the postoffice played a small part in my life. I was content to get mail on an average of perhaps once a week. The children's departure changed that. I wanted my mail every day, and in summer, at least, I managed to get it. Sometimes I drove all those miles for nothing more than a newspaper or a magazine, but I didn't mind. One letter repaid me for several trips to town.

The postoffice is a favorite gathering-place for all the Valley in summer. No railroad runs into this end of the Valley, and five o'clock finds many of us awaiting the mail stage that comes over the mountains from Butte. When the stage is late, we have an excuse to linger and talk, to discuss the latest developments on the war front, the labor situation, the fishing, the coming barn dance at one of the big dude ranches and that good old standby, the weather.

Mrs. Chowning, our postmistress, likes to have us con-
gregate in the postoffice. She's the kindest, friendliest, most
understanding soul in this Valley. She knows every one of
us, both dude and native, intimately, and her friendliness
dates back to a day when friendship meant sharing of good
luck or bad luck; of joy or sorrow. As a child she came over
the plains in a covered wagon. Her father, an Old-Timer,
founded our small valley town, which still bears his name.
He was the first postmaster, and for the almost half-century
since his death she has carried on in his place.

We are not exactly a big happy family, waiting for the
mail; our interests and backgrounds are too widely divergent for that. But the postoffice is a sort of melting-pot,
just the same, where a giant ladle stirs the natives with the
dudes.

In the small enclosure this side of the mailboxes and on
the broad walk outside, rancher, bartender, cowboy or
herder, merchant, waitress or beauty operator, at some time
or other will rub elbows with celebrities from Outside ... a
Metropolitan Opera star, a world-renowned surgeon, a
famous author or playwright, a nationally known business
executive — even the nobility of distant lands.

The old frame building which housed the first valley postoffice is still in use and bursting at the seams. There is a
startled lift to its eaves and its windows have the apologetic
look of an underfed child who has gorged himself on a pil-
fered jam-pot. Our postoffice was originally built to care
for less than one hundred people. Why wouldn't it be flab-
bergasted when forced, in dude season, to cancel mail for
six times that many?

The initiated could tell the native from the dude at a
glance, but a stranger would have to look closely. The line
is thinly drawn in the case of the younger fry. They dress

much alike, the difference in rare instances being a matter
of quality: the difference between 'store-bought' boots and
custom-mades, between hand-tailored shirts and 'boughten'
ones. The levis of the young people are identical. Made of
stout blue denim, they cost approximately two dollars and
were most likely bought at the same shop, two doors up the
street.

The distinguishing line is sharper in women of my generation. I blush to admit that those of us who live here
twelve months of the year are behind the times, for we still
wear dresses. The dudes of that age, and older, wear pants.
We are perfectly aware that trousers are the comfortable,
sensible garb for this country. The dudes have convinced
us. But the dudes have not looked at overalls, laundered
overalls and patched overalls, every day of a hard, shut-in
winter, and we have.

I don't know when the first dude came into this Valley.
It was a long time ago and nobody seems to be quite certain
of the date. Perhaps this is because we did not recognize
the dude as a dude. Perhaps he was some visitor who liked
it so well that he went back East and told his friends about
our isolated Valley, where the hunting and fishing is second
to none. At any rate it was in the depression years, after
1929, that the dude became a definite factor in our lives.
Many stockmen were merely eking out an existence at the
time, and when they looked about for some means of increasing their incomes, the dudes were waiting.

The stockmen were not prepared to take care of them,
and suddenly one spring there was a flurry of building. The
Forest resounded to the ring of the axe and the drone of the
crosscut saw. All over the state ranchers began erecting
small log cabins. They advertised for dudes, and got them
too, at prices that seemed fabulous to me. They weren't

fabulous, considering. The dudes were feeling the pinch of the depression as well as we. They wanted to retrench, and the cost of vacationing on a Montana stock ranch was negligible when compared with the cost of a summer on the Continent.

A number of dudes came into the Valley and I got a notion I'd like to take in a few. We already had several small log cabins on our place and these could be repaired and furnished with a small cash outlay. The more thought I gave to the matter, the more attractive it became. The back of an envelope and a well-sharpened pencil is all I need to figure a profit. It's one of my favorite diversions and Tom, in the past, had always been able to dampen my enthusiasm by pointing out some figures I'd forgotten to set down. I was determined to be ready and I computed the cost of taking in dudes to the last saddle and bridle, the last towel and washcloth, before I spoke of my scheme. When an opportunity presented itself, I decided on the forthright approach.

'Tom,' I said, 'let's fix up our cabins and take in some dudes.'

Not one muscle of his face moved, but I could sense his solid resistance. 'I'm a sheepman,' he announced flatly, 'and sheep and dudes won't mix.'

'How do you know they won't?' I argued, taken aback. This was a line I was not prepared for. I had armed myself with figures and I was running into facts. 'How do you know? You've never tried to mix them. Dudes would be easy to care for. They wouldn't stray off like sheep or pile up in the river.'

'That's what you think,' he replied with a deceptive calm. 'You can't cast your line into the river any more without hooking a dude in the seat of the pants.'

I giggled in spite of myself. 'Just because you caught your fishhook *once* in a dude's pants!'

'That's only a sample. Look what they've done to the town. I tried to buy a pair of bib overalls for a herder today. I didn't get them. The clerk told me they seldom had calls for anything but waist overalls any more. *The dudes prefer waist overalls.* That's the size of it. I suppose it's up to the rest of us to change over or go naked.'

'If you can't lick 'em, jine 'em,' I said. 'They're here to stay. The merchants are smart. They're falling into line.'

'All right. Let them stay, but let them stay in the commercial dude camps. They're prepared to take care of them and we aren't.' That was the end of my fine scheme. We never took in a dude, and I've always been sorry....

In those days I had a fixed conception of a dude. When I was a child there was a dude of the old school in our family circle, an uncle who wore spats and carried a cane, who attended church on Sunday mornings in a tall silk hat, pin-striped gray trousers and frock-coat. Unconsciously I carried that picture in my mind each time I thought of a dude.

I shall never forget the first one I ever saw in this country. He outcowboyed the cowboy from underslung boots to sweat-stained Stetson. He wore an ornate pair of chaps and a shirt so violently red that I felt the need of blinkers. His gold-embossed spurs clinked jauntily when he swaggered up the street. I'm afraid I gaped at all this splendor, for the dude was abreast of me before I could drag my fascinated eyes to his face. He grinned, his teeth forming white arcs in what must have been a week's growth of beard. As I watched him stroll down the street, I felt sorry for the barber and wondered if he hadn't been too optimistic when he installed a second chair in his shop.

Until the dudes came we paid little attention to the pic-

turesqueness of our raiment. We did not dress to give color
to our background. When we ran across a Western story
in which the hero wore a ten-gallon hat, brilliant scarf and
all the trappings, we read it with our tongues in our cheeks.

The top cowhands in our Valley wore ordinary hats and
any kind of clothes that came near to their hand. They
donned chaps when they needed them, as a protection
against cold in winter, against brush and timber in summer,
and they took them off gratefully the moment they got into
the bunkhouse.

The dudes changed all that. They had a definite idea of
what the well-dressed cowhand should wear, and presently,
on dress parade at least, our cowboys began to live up to
that picture. When I gleefully pointed this out to Tom, he
said:

'Well — there's a law against going naked. They have
to buy what they find in the stores.'

But he was wrong and he knew it. Cowboys like color and
swank. They send all over the United States and Canada
for their spurs and chaps, their shirts and boots and hats.
I'd be willing to wager that you couldn't search through any
cattle outfit bunkhouse without running across a half-dozen
or more catalogues put out by firms which specialize in cowboy outfits. And those catalogues will be dog-eared and
falling apart from constant handling.

We underestimated the dudes when they first came. I'm
afraid we grudgingly thought of them as a necessary intrusion that would pass when times got better. Well, times
have been better several times, and the dudes are still here
and they increase in number with each succeeding summer.

We underestimated the courage of those first dudes. I
remember one, a lad of nineteen, whose urban pallor was
shocking to eyes grown used to healthy Montana bronze.

He looked positively ill, and I should have thought that the first horse he mounted would 'dust' him promptly. Yet for sheer grit and endurance, this lad might have put a seasoned rider to shame.

The cowboy of that day resented the dude, and held him in poor esteem. He was hired to wrangle cattle, he proclaimed loudly to all who would listen, *not dudes*. He'd be derned if he'd play nurse to a dude. In some cases he had to, or hunt another job. But he felt a mean advantage had been taken of him, and he slyly retaliated by baiting the intruders.

Tall tales spread over the Valley of practical jokes that resulted in dudes' being taken down a peg or two. But there were other tales, equally amusing, that did not get around. One cowboy who possessed a sense of humor so keen that he could enjoy a joke on himself told me a curious story. It concerned the pale-faced lad I have just mentioned. He came out to the corral on the day of his arrival and asked for a horse. The cowboy took one look at him and saddled an old swaybacked white mare. The dude was indignant.

'I asked for a *horse*, and I'd like something with a little spirit,' he announced haughtily.

The cowboy kept his temper because the germ of what seemed a fitting revenge was mulling about in his brain. Among the horses in the corral there was a little gelding which had a spirited lift to his head and dancing restless feet. He looked like a bronc, but he was really as harmless as a lamb. He had one bad habit. So long as the reins were held snugly a child could handle him; but leave one inch of slack in the reins and he would spill his rider and leap out into space.

The cowboy saddled and led the gelding forth. He was

enjoying himself enormously now. He took hold of the bit while the dude mounted and handed over the reins with a decided slack in their length. Before the lad could straighten the slack the cowboy let go of the bit. The gelding laid back his ears, snorted, jumped into the air and landed running.

The dude did not know the meaning of 'pulling leather,' but he learned it suddenly. With frantic fingers he clutched at the reins, the saddle-horn, the horse's mane — anything in fact that he could get a grip on. His body only made connection with the saddle a time or two before the gelding disappeared over the top of a low hill.

The cowboy was chastened and dismayed. It had tickled his fancy to humble the lad with a prompt, painful 'dusting' near the corrals, and now he had visions of his victim being thrown on some steep rocky hillside by a horse over which he had no control. He flung himself on another horse and followed. The best part of an hour elapsed before he found the dude, and when he ran onto him he could scarcely believe his eyes. The lad was a little white about the mouth and had lost his hat, but he was still astride his mount. He had learned the trick of the reins too, for the gelding was trotting along docilely.

'Have any trouble?' the cowboy gulped.

The dude glared at him suspiciously for a moment and then he began to laugh. 'When they shed me,' he boasted, 'they have to shed their hides.'

The spectacular courage of some of the dudes all but defeated the stockman who had taken them in. In his simplicity the rancher had thought to feed and lodge the dude and furnish him with a gentle horse. He had expected then to dismiss him from his mind and go about his business as usual.

It was rather a jolt when he discovered that this was exactly what he couldn't do. He was responsible for the dude's safety as well as his observance of the unwritten laws, of which Montana had many. He couldn't let his guests ride alone because there was nothing they wouldn't try once. For instance, many of the mountains surrounding this valley are dangerous to climb. The rock walls from a distance look solid enough, but they are really honeycombed and break away when the least pressure is put upon them. Many are so dangerous that no native, be he ever so bold, will attempt to scale them. Yet dudes have scaled them. That they are still alive to tell the story is a matter of blind luck and nothing more.

There are trails into our timbered mountains so narrow and treacherous that the dislodging of one rock could easily hurl a horse and rider to their death a thousand feet below. The men who live in this valley and know every stone and badger hole will detour for miles to miss these trails. Yet dudes have tried them out with utter disregard for life and limb.

The baffled, harried rancher, unable to leave his business at a busy season of the year, was forced to hire a rider to accompany the dudes on their trips into the mountains and thus the word 'dude wrangler' was coined. But he soon found that one wrangler was not enough. He needed several, because no two groups of dudes could ever be persuaded to take the same trip.

These wranglers 'rode herd' on the more adventurous dudes, but those dudes who were content to roam over the countryside were permitted to ride alone. This too was a mistake. Soon the rancher, who was already beginning to have doubts about the dude business, began to be besieged from all sides by wrathful, protesting neighbors. Dudes had

ignored unwritten laws; they had left gates open, they had
eaten in a sheep wagon or cow camp and failed to wash up
the dishes afterward. And those who owned cars had raced
through herds of sheep or cattle on the country road, leaving confusion and havoc in their wake.

The old-time Montanan seldom gives advice. He didn't
now, but he taxed his story-telling powers to the limit. He'd
say at the table: 'Can't see why there's so much wind this
time of year. Hope the gate into my alfalfa is fast. It blows
open sometimes.' And then he'd tell about the time four of
his registered milch cows had found an open gate, wandered
into alfalfa and died of bloat.

Or he might amuse his listeners with the tale of the
herder who shot a certain trapper through the wrist. 'The
trapper had it coming,' the rancher would explain to his
wide-eyed guests. 'He was trapping close to this herder's
wagon. He'd go in at noon, while the herder was out with
his sheep, and cook himself some grub. And then — *he'd
walk right off and leave his greasy dishes.* He deserved what
he got.'

This story is a favorite of mine, so I shall finish it. When
hailed before the judge and accused, the sheepherder said:
'Sure, I winged him. There ain't no law against protectin'
yourself, is there? I warned him. I left notes all over the
wagon, but every night I had to wash his dirty dishes. Well,
I laid for him and I fixed him so's he won't be cookin' grub in
nobody's wagon for a spell.' The judge, who was also a retired sheepman, is supposed then to have dismissed the
case, and berated the hapless trapper in such a fashion that
he slunk out of court.

The rancher told a lot of stories before he got his points
across. Most of our unwritten laws appealed to the dudes,
because they had a tang of the old West. As time went on

they rather prided themselves on the fact that they knew and respected them, and they held in contempt and disfavor any dude who refused to do the same. But the closing of gates was a hard one to take. The dudes thought of this country as a place of wide-open spaces where their freedom was limited only by the number of miles they could ride horseback in a day. They hated gates and they hated fences, and I can't say I blame them. I hate gates too, but I've learned that they are necessary.

By the end of the first dude season the rancher had things well in hand. His neighbors were speaking to him again and his dudes were still sound of limb. But his troubles were not over. A third type of dude began to seek accommodation at his ranch — the helpful dude. The helpful dude had no yen to ride in timbered mountains, nor did he care to risk his shins on the slippery boulders of our swift fishing streams. In the beginning this type of dude seemed nothing short of a gift from the gods. He was content to stay close to the ranch and the rancher. Too close, as it later transpired.

The helpful dude was dallying with the idea of buying a ranch of his own. He wanted to learn the livestock business from the ground up. He was constantly underfoot, firing question after question at his disillusioned host, insisting that he take part in all the ranch activities. He was always on hand when there were cattle to be rounded up and cut out, when there were sheep to be moved. He was clumsy and ineffectual and his ignorance of the habits of livestock resulted in the loss of much time, in confusion and errors.

One rancher said to me: 'They were always around. The only way I could shed them was to get them started on some chore that didn't matter and then sneak out and do my work.' But even this ended in near tragedy, the rancher

informed me, because he ran out of jobs and had to invent
one. He suggested one morning that two of the dudes dig
a post hole to replace a rotting telephone pole quite close to
the house. The day was warm, and when the dudes had
shoveled a hole that was scarcely deep enough for a hen to
dust herself comfortably in, their zeal began to diminish.

The day before they had watched one of the irrigators
blow up a beaver's dam with a stick of dynamite. It occurred to the dudes that this method of digging would save
a lot of time. They secured a stick of dynamite, placed it in
the shallow hole, tamped it down with mud and put a huge
boulder on top. The post hole was a success, but the
boulder skyrocketed several hundred feet into the air and
came down through the roof of the ranch house just five
minutes after the rancher's wife had quitted the room in
which it landed.

I honestly believe that it was the helpful dude who
caused most of the livestock dude ranches in our Valley to
fold up. The ranchers deny it. They claim that times improved and the necessity ceased to exist. But I know the
sheepman, at least, well enough to be certain that he can
take anything so long as it does not threaten the welfare of
his business — and that he cannot take.

Nevertheless, the dudes have had their place in our lives
and they have taught us many things. They have jerked us
up by the scruff of the neck, jolted us out of our rut and
taught us a new way of living. They have brought glamor
into our lives and new blood and a certain restlessness that
has proved a spur to our endeavors.

They have taught us to appreciate the lofty grandeur of
our mountain ranges, the beauty of our swift and turbulent
streams — things we have been wont to take for granted.
We can thank the dudes for the miles of smooth oiled high-

ways that connect our Valley with the world outside. We
owe them many things and we like them now and understand them as they have come to understand us. But we
like them best in the commercial ranches which are operated
for their benefit alone. These ranches are equipped to take
care of the dude and his problems — and we are not.

20

Mountain Lilies

FROM the time Wezie was a very small girl she had wanted to own a wild horse. When she outgrew Patches, her pinto Welsh pony, she spoke of it first. Tom had been looking for a likely horse to replace Patches, found one that pleased him and offered to take Wezie to look him over.

She was an independent, determined little person and she replied: 'I've already picked out the pony I want. He's a Mountain Lily. Bill Anderson roped him up Dry Hollow and broke him last spring. And Daddy,'—there was awe in her vibrant young voice — 'I'm sure he's kin to Son of Satan. He's coal black with a white star on his forehead!'

Tom flung me an accusing, reproachful glance and settled down to dissuade this child who could twist him around her finger. The Mountain Lilies were inbred and often mean, he told Wezie, not the sort of horseflesh a rancher cares to run with the good stock on his place. He brought forth other arguments, but he might as well have begged the wind not to blow. He was licked from the start, though he held out for weeks. He gave in on the eve of Wezie's eleventh birthday and brought the black horse to the ranch.

I had been firmly aligned on Wezie's side and it was just as well that I was, for I should have got the blame anyway. It was I who had told her bedtime stories about Son of Satan since she was old enough to remember; it was I who had taught her to love the outlaw Kentucky stallion which joined up with a herd of wild horses and outsmarted a half-dozen early settlers over a number of years.

Wezie loved the black pony as she loved no other one possession. She tried to call him Son of Satan. Unfortunately, Bill Anderson had already dubbed him Nig, and as so often happens, the name stuck. But just the same, in Wezie's secret heart of hearts, all the splendor and courage and intelligence of that thoroughbred stallion lived on in the far from glamorous cow pony which was Nig. It was something I could never understand. She was not a fanciful child. She was as direct and down to earth as Tom, far more so than either of the boys. She did not tell me of her fancy but I felt it. I never saw her sturdy, gallant little figure with flying hair and a back-flung grin gallop away on Nig that my mind did not call up an imagined picture of Son of Satan, his shining mane outflung — thundering hoofs racing before the wind to elude his pursuers.

There are still wild horses in our mountains. I have seen them often, silhouetted sharply against the skyline on some distant rocky crest. Ugly, short-legged little beasts with overlarge heads and stocky ungraceful bodies. Inbred, stubborn and mean, incongruously named Mountain Lilies by some early settler who had a perverted sense of humor, and still called that.

Wild horses ... Mountain Lilies ... the very words excited my interest when I first came to Montana. Nobody seemed to know much about their origin — and cared less. I learned that they had ranged the mountains as long as anyone remembered. Every decade or so, when they became numerous enough to overgraze the range, the ranchers got together, rounded them up and shipped them to the packers. Infrequently they bred a throwback, a good saddle horse, which was cut out from their ranks and broken. Nig was one of these.

I was bitterly disappointed the first time I saw a herd of wild horses. I spoke of it later to one of our Old-Timers.

'Mountain Lilies!' I exclaimed. 'Why, they're hideous — grotesque travesties — really.'

A twinkle danced across the Old-Timer's eyes. 'They weren't always so,' he brought out quickly. 'There was good stuff for a while — when Son of Satan led the herds. There still is occasionally.'

With a little persuasion he told me the story then.

The Mountain Lilies had caught the interest of one of the early settlers. He decided that, properly bred, the mares might bring good cow-ponies, and to try out his theory he imported a beautiful thoroughbred stallion from his home state of Kentucky. He awaited an opportunity and drove the stallion into a herd of Mountain Lilies, believing it would be a simple matter to corral the herd later, cut out his stallion and the new crop of colts he had sired.

He was mistaken. The stallion adopted all the Lilies on

the range and became wilder than any of them. His superior intelligence made him a natural leader and he ranged with one herd and then another, making it impossible to identify him with any certain herd. Again and again his owner attempted to run him down and corral him, only to meet with defeat. The stallion knew every trail through the timber, every rocky inaccessible peak, and with diabolical cunning he refused to let himself and his herd be maneuvered into any corner from which there was no escape.

The rancher spent the best part of two summers trying to corral him, but he finally gave up and wrote the stallion off as a loss. Several years passed. In these years the rancher had accumulated a good herd of work and saddle horses. When there were too many to range on his ranch, he turned them into the hills for winter grazing. One spring he drove them in as usual to cut out some work teams and was dismayed to discover that two of his best brood mares were missing. He rode for days but could find no trace of them.

Some weeks later a prospector told him he had seen two branded mares in a wild herd which the stallion was leading. This was too much. The rancher called on his neighbors for help, and no posse ever trailed a rustler so furiously as those ranchers trailed the stallion.

The old gentleman who told me the story took part in the hunt. With many a chuckle he related how the stallion had tricked them. 'That rascal enjoyed it,' he said, 'and led us a merry chase. Some days he'd encourage us; let us run him till our horses played out and we had to turn back ... Seemed like he was afraid we'd give up and spoil his fun. He'd let us drive his herd into narrow ravines, from which we'd have sworn he couldn't escape. But the moment we started to close in, he'd kick up his heels, whinny the Lilies to follow and leap up some hidden trail in the timber.'

Repeated defeat discouraged the ranchers, the Old-Timer said. They had other things to do. They sympathized with the stallion's owner, but they could neglect their work no longer. Riding back from a long, fruitless race one rancher said, 'I hope you catch that son of Satan and I'd like to be in on it, but I'm too busy to ride any more.' This was not the name set down on the stallion's papers, but it stuck. Son of Satan, he was called from that day.

One by one the ranchers dropped out, but the following spring the stallion's owner did not lack company, for the pick of all the branded mares on the range joined up with Son of Satan's wild herd. The ranchers rode forth again with grim determination. Time after time the wily Son of Satan and his Lilies eluded them. This was a challenge to the settler's skill and ingenuity and all were equally involved. The quest took on the quality of a crusade. The ranchers no longer hoped to corral the stallion. They agreed among themselves that the first man who got within rifle range of the animal should let him have it.

This was not so simple a matter, as they soon found out. The wild herd now counted many fine mares among its number and these stuck close to the stallion in whichever herd he ranged. On the infrequent occasions when a rancher got close enough to take aim, the mares got in his way. The settlers matched cunning with cunning. They studied the stallion's habits. They figured he'd lead his herd to certain waterholes or springs at midday if the weather was dry, but might not show up for days on end if it rained. They discovered that the stallion preferred to graze on bunch grass and would pass up sections of wild timothy, which narrowed their field of operation. They would lie in wait near these waterholes or in favored grass sections, and would wait in vain. For on the days they had chosen, the stallion remained away.

Another year passed and still the stallion ran free on the range. Ranchers with only one mare in the wild herd acknowledged defeat and again dropped out. Son of Satan, however, had kidnapped three of the Old-Timer's mares. They were valuable animals and he refused to give up. He rode when he had the time, and never went out on the range without his rifle. One day his persistence was rewarded.

It was early spring and the snow was still deep on the ground. The Old-Timer had been half-heartedly following the trail of a single horse. He had figured that since the stallion ranged with different herds there was bound to be a time, between herds, when he ranged alone. In the pursuit of this notion, he had followed single trails before, only to come upon a branded stray in the end. When he dropped over the crest of a hill, he could hardly believe his luck.

Son of Satan was down, thrashing savagely about in a huge drift. His body and head were frosted with snow and his sides were heaving from his exertions. The Old-Timer dismounted and edged cautiously closer to determine the cause of the stallion's disaster. The horse's hoof was caught fast in the loose wire of a fence! This portion of the fence always drifted under in winter. It took but a second for the Old-Timer to piece out the story. The stallion, accustomed to running over the hard, crusted surface, had been betrayed by the season. The snow became soft in the spring. The drift had broken under his weight and in his struggles to right himself his hoof had been trapped.

The Old-Timer experienced a moment of triumph. He moved over in line with the desperately struggling creature's head, got down on his knees and took aim ...

At this point my friend stopped short and looked out toward the mountains, those green, shining mountains where Son of Satan had ranged. There was a strange exalted expression in his faded blue eyes, and as I stared, repulsed and disillusioned, a whimsical smile crept up about the corners of his mouth.

How could you? I thought. How could you shoot that horse and like to do it!

'I couldn't do it!' he brought out slowly, as though he had read my mind. 'I could no more have shot that horse than I could have shot my wife. God! If you could have seen his eyes! The way he quit fighting, lay still for a minute and then raised his head and looked me square in the face . . . like he was saying, "*It was a good game while it lasted, but you won.*"

'I found me a tree stump, sat down and did some thinking. I knew I'd have to leave the country if I turned him loose . . . and I'd feel like a skunk the rest of my life if I roped him whilst he was down. For the life of me I couldn't shoot him.' He turned to me with a chuckle. 'Know what I did? I set him free.'

I let my breath out slowly and relaxed in my chair. We sat in silence for a long moment and then I asked, 'What did the ranchers think about it?'

He chuckled again. 'They were pleased, and I'm right proud of the way I handled it. I turned that horse loose and we never had any trouble corralling him after that. His owner got a dozen or more good colts from the Lilies every year the stallion lived, and every mare he kidnapped brought a good colt too.'

I'm gullible, but this was a little too much for me to swallow. 'He permitted you to corral him because you had spared his life?' I asked with what I hoped was a touch of irony.

The Old-Timer smiled and shook his head. 'No — that wasn't the way of it. Son of Satan just naturally lost his taste for speed, and I'll tell you how I cured him. Several days before, I'd picked up a horseshoe on the range. It was still in my saddlebags. I got it out and tied it to the stallion's forelock before I set him free. Every time that rascal got out of a trot, the horseshoe bounced up and down against his skull and knocked some sense into his feet.'

2 I

The children

THROUGHOUT the depression, in fact until Leigh and Andy were ready for high school, the children attended the small district school five miles from the ranch. For several years I drove them back and forth, though my services were far from welcome. They wanted to ride horseback in fair weather, as the rest of the pupils did. It set them apart and embarrassed them no end to have their mother drive up to the door and deliver them like so many packages.

The children rode well, had practically lived in the saddle for most of their lives. The back of a horse was as familiar to Leigh and Andy and Wezie as a chair might be to some city child. A five-mile jaunt to school was nothing, they insisted. But each time I thought of the short cut they'd take beyond the canyon, my courage failed.

The worst of it was that I couldn't discuss the matter

frankly. I had to hedge and evade. I couldn't cry out, 'I'm afraid — afraid you'll lose your way in a sudden storm, afraid your horses might shy and throw you — that you'll be hurt and die of exposure before help can be got.' I simply could not stand up to the picture of three pairs of eyes regarding me with pity or with scorn.

Of course I never fooled them. They knew I was afraid, and it was this knowledge and the fear of hurting me which held them in leash. I was still a poor horsewoman and would always be. Every saddle horse I dared to mount knew it and took unfair advantage. If I wanted a horse to trot, he promptly broke into a gallop; if I wanted him to gallop he walked or went round in a circle. Horses to me were irritating, unpredictable creatures; I'd never seen one I felt I could put my faith in. And my children still seemed such babies.

Babies? They were older than I in many ways — in knowledge of livestock, of trail and sign lore and of weather. And fear was not in them.

Each fall I counted the days until the weather should become so bad that there'd be no question of riding horseback to school and the matter could be shelved until spring. Frankly, I had no idea I was working a hardship on them, but I found that was true.

One afternoon in late October I drove up to the school and honked the horn. The children emerged promptly and their faces were unnaturally sober. One part of my mind took this in but the other part almost rejected the sight before me. Leigh's shirt was half torn off him and one eye was badly discolored: Andy's lip was cut and swollen and his clothes were caked with mud. Little Wezie, trotting along between her brothers, presented a disconcerting picture. One pigtail of fair hair had come unbraided and was flying about in the wind, her tie was askew, the knee of one stocking was out and the other hung down over her oxford, with the garter flapping on the ground. The teacher fluttered along in their wake.

My battle-scarred trio climbed sheepishly into the car as the teacher broke into incoherent speech.

'Andy started this,' she stuttered. 'I saw him jump on Jimmie from the window. Before I could get outdoors all three of them had Jimmie down.'

Jimmie I knew to be the bully of the school; he was sixteen and would make two of Andy. There was something queer about this. Andy was impetuous and hot-tempered but he wasn't a fool. It had taken something pretty dreadful to make him forget Jimmie's size and brawn. I turned in my seat and regarded the culprit.

'What did Jimmie do?' I demanded in a voice which I'm afraid was not as stern as it should have been.

'Yes, what did he do?' the teacher broke in. 'That's what I've been trying to find out for the past hour.'

'Well, Andrew?'

My son's face went sulky. 'He didn't do anything. I just don't like him.'

And that was all he would say, that was all any of them would say until Tom got the story out of Wezie that night. Jimmie had called Andy a sissy. 'Just like your ma,' he had teased. 'If I bounced up and down in a saddle like your ma does, I'd stay off a horse. I'd come to school in a car too.' And Wezie had warned: 'Don't tell Mother. It would hurt her feelings. She can't help bouncing.'

That settled it. In fair weather they rode horseback to school thereafter. They never had an accident, they never got caught in one of the swift, terrifying storms that so often overtake us in this valley. But just the same I never saw them set out down the canyon that I did not breathe a silent prayer for their safe return, that I did not long to ride after them — to protect them from I knew not what. It was strange. I wanted them to be independent, to stand alone, to face valiantly the Jimmies of their world. And yet, somehow, I wanted them to need me too ... something still tugged at the apron-strings of my heart.

Leigh was the scholar. He loved to study and took a keen delight in his work. Andy had a quick, brilliant mind that could grasp a subject instantly and see it through to its source, but he loathed the daily grind and had to be driven to his books. Andy, naturally, came in for a lot of scolding which Leigh escaped.

The two boys, so near an age, were devoted, in spite of the difference in disposition and habits. Leigh was methodical, tidy, and could be trusted to do well any task he was given. Andy performed tasks outside the house with surprising efficiency but when an emergency arose indoors, he always had business elsewhere. If I pinned him down and forced him to a job I had to stand over him to make sure he'd do it well, or even finish it. This exasperated me and baffled me too. I couldn't figure out why Andy could clean a barn, a shed or a chickenhouse with facility and dispatch, and yet be so careless and slow when told to tidy his room or sweep down the stairs.

I hadn't time to stand guard, and consequently if I wanted a job done quickly and well, I called on Leigh. Andy had me buffaloed until I overheard a bit of conversation which took place one day while Leigh was sweeping the stairs.

'I always get this job when a cook leaves,' Leigh grumbled, 'and I'm getting tired of it. Mom never asks you any more.'

I was conscience-stricken, for Leigh told the truth. For some reason that was not quite clear in my mind I decided that I'd rather not have the boys know I'd been eavesdropping and had begun to tiptoe out of the room when I heard Andy's chuckle: 'You know why, don't you? You do it too good. Next time do it any-which-way and she won't ask you any more.'

I stepped into the hall and confronted them. Without a word I took the broom from Leigh and handed it to Andy. Thereafter I had only to warn that I wanted a job done well — not any-which-way — and Andy did it well.

When the boys started to high school and had to live away from home, we engaged a tutor for Wezie. For two years she attended school at the ranch. She had always loved Stonyacres and in these years that love deepened immeasurably. There was never a time when she wanted to leave. Often I'd try to sound her out about high school or college and she always replied: 'Mother, I'm not going to college — or even high school — if I have to leave home. I want to stay here.'

There is not a foot of the ranch that does not carry its picture of Wezie. Wezie, climbing the hill with a gun over her shoulder and dogs at her heels. Wezie, galloping away on Nig. Wezie, on skis, skimming down some steep, snowy slope with the effortless ease of a bird. . . .

Meanwhile the boys were finishing their education, partly in Montana, and partly in Texas. Their vacations were never satisfying; always seemed too brief. Almost before we realized how the years had passed, Leigh took a position in California, and Andy found one in Texas. Presently they married — girls I knew and loved. They have done well in their work and both hold responsible positions in distant cities, but we seldom see them now.

Recently, as I drove through a field on my way to the Thayer ranch, I saw two of the Thayer boys irrigating a stand of alfalfa. For a moment an old familiar ache took hold of me — Mr. Thayer's boys were near. He could see them every day. Our boys ... I told myself I mustn't think about it. But I had no sooner crossed the Thayer threshold than I cried out impulsively, 'You don't know how lucky you are having your boys always with you.'

Before I got the words out of my mouth I knew what Mr. Thayer's reply would be. I had brought it on myself.

'"Tain't luck,' he contradicted flatly. 'We sent our boys to Montana schools — like some folks didn't. They hitched up with Montana girls and stayed where they belong.'

But Mr. Thayer was wrong. My daughters-in-law were not to blame ... the schools were not to blame. It was just one of those things that happen ... that can't be helped. If I hadn't been certain before I was convinced of it now.

Leigh came home for one of his rare visits this summer. On the day he was to leave we climbed to the top of the grade and stood arm in arm looking over the broad fertile acres. Across the valley the last rays of a setting sun brushed the snowclad peak of Old Sugar Loaf, Leigh's favorite mountain, with crimson and gold.

We stood there for a long time, silent, watching the sunset fade and grow dim. Presently I raised my eyes to my tall son's face and saw a familiar betraying muscle quiver near the corner of his mouth.

'There's nothing like it — anywhere,' he brought out slowly, and his next words told it all: 'Oh, Mother! Why couldn't Dad have run cattle instead of sheep? Andy and I like cattle.'

Wezie never left the ranch. Before that time came she

died — after a four days' illness. I cannot talk or write
about it yet ... I cannot think of her as dead. For death
means extinction and Wezie's spirit, the vivid, gallant spirit
of a happy little girl, lives on. I never hear the sound of
galloping hoofs that I do not call up a picture of Wezie on
her black horse Nig ... that I do not find myself listening
for her vibrant young voice ... her merry laugh.

The creek winds away from the house, the slope of the
hills climb up out of sight, the land stretches off into limit-
less space. ... And perhaps ... somewhere on this ranch ...

22

Water

OUR haying is done and we had a good crop this year. For weeks each time I've taken drinking water to the men in the hayfields I've filled my lungs with the pungent sweetness of new-mown hay. I've watched the shining blades of the mowers plow through a carpet of purple and green; the clattering dump rakes drag the cured swath into tidy windrows — then bunch these symmetrically; the plodding bull rakes pick up the bunches and trip their loads on the stacks. It has been good for my soul, and now the two miles of hay meadow which lie between the home ranch and the big red gate on the county road are dotted with haystacks.

I'm sure no miser ever gloated over his gold or counted his riches with more satisfaction than the woolgrower of

the Northwest experiences when he measures up a good
crop of hay.

I helped Tom measure his hay yesterday. Arithmetic
has never been one of my strong points, but when Tom casts
the steel tape over a stack I can reel it from its metal casing
and call out the figures which he marks down in his little
black book.

I'd hate to compute the number of tons from those figures, however. Some ewe would surely go hungry. My
errors in calculation have a bad way of galloping ahead;
they never lag behind. Tom can't understand this and he
has long since ceased trying. But in his heart he's convinced that all Texans are given to superlatives. My family
are, at any rate, and that's quite enough for Tom. He's
hardened to it, but he can never resist giving me a dig
when I stretch things a little. For instance, if I say, 'I
waited hours for you in the pouring rain,' he is sure to reply,
'You waited exactly forty-five minutes, and it didn't rain
hard enough to lay the dust.'

Yesterday afternoon he called me down mildly. There
were one hundred and thirty butts of hay to measure.
When we finished the last one he sat down on the running-
board of the truck and figured up the number of tons in
our crop. His voice was matter-of-fact as he told me the
grand total, but his eyes betrayed his elation.

'Why, that's a bumper crop!' I exclaimed in an awed
voice.

'It's not a bumper crop,' he corrected firmly, but added
with a grin, 'It's a darn good one, though.'

A few moments later he said, 'I'd rather have hay in the
stack than money in the bank.' And *this* was no extrava-
gant statement. It was the truth.

What woolgrower wouldn't rather have hay in the stack

than money in the bank? So long as the woolgrower has good sound ewes, he can find the money to run them. They are his gilt-edged security upon which he can borrow to the limit of their current market value. If prices are normal or better, his lambs will take care of all his obligations at the end of the year, and his wool will represent his profit. If prices are poor, he may have to throw his wool in with his lambs to meet his bills. But he still has his breeding ewes which are his stock in trade. If he is wise it behooves him to keep them in excellent condition, for the size of his lamb crop and the quality of his clip of wool depends upon how well he has wintered his ewes.

When the woolgrower's hay crop falls far below standard, a fat bank account will not solve his difficulties. Nine times out of ten, if his hay is not adequate for his needs, his neighbors will be facing the same problem. Hay cannot be bought for any price in this valley when there's a general shortage. Money lying idle in the bank won't always buy security for a flock, but a plentiful hay crop will.

To make sure that there will be hay in the stack there must also be water in the ditches. And now we come to the fundamental by which we stand or fall, the life-blood and backbone of the livestock industry in Montana — *water*.

Practically all the cultivated land in this part of the state is under ditch. Except in rare instances dry-land crops have proved too uncertain to depend upon. Rainfall ensures good grazing but it seldom comes in sufficient quantity to penetrate the earth to the deep tough roots of the alfalfa. Only hours of skillful surface flooding can accomplish that.

Most of the ditches in this part of the country are taken out of creeks that are fed from small springs and the melting snow in the mountains. The springs are not sufficient;

there must be snow in the mountains if those creeks are to carry an adequate supply of water for irrigation.

It is not hard to understand, then, why the woolgrower can plunge through snow that reaches past his horse's belly and never complain; why he can shovel drifts that take toll of his strength and patience and do it cheerfully. He can put up with the cold and discomfort and exposure because he knows in his heart that if there is snow on the lower levels of his range, there will be still more snow in the mountains.

Men have fought and died, paid heavy fines, served jail sentences and nourished lifelong grudges in Montana — for water or its lack. This never-ending war has existed since the second rancher in the Territory took a ditch out of a stream which the first rancher claimed for his own.

In pioneer days the first settler who took water out of a stream for irrigation was entitled by Territory law to the first right for as much water as he needed to irrigate his land properly. The second and third settlers had the same privilege, and so on down the line until there was no longer any water in the stream.

The violently argued and bitterly contested question was just how much water each settler did need for the proper irrigation of his land. The flexibility of what really constituted the proper use of water was definitely at fault in those days. No account was taken of the individual efficiency of the irrigators, which was a mistake. (Right here on this ranch I have known a poor irrigator to take two hundred inches of water to irrigate a field, where a good irrigator had never before used more than a hundred inches.) If the settler with the second right happened to be a conscientious, careful irrigator and the settler with the first right a careless one, the feud was on.

For another thing, the first settler may have established his water right in a year when the streams overflowed. If water got scarce, he continued to flood his fields extravagantly. There were always times when he could have turned water back into the stream, but he was afraid a precedent might be established, so he kept it jealously down to the last inch he was allowed by law. The crops of the second rancher, in a dry year, would suffer, while the third rancher might find himself with no water at all.

The second rancher with insufficient water and the third rancher with none did not take to this state of affairs. Hot words and threats were exchanged which only resulted in the first rancher's irrigating his crops with a pistol on his hip. The second and third ranchers valued their skins, but they valued their crops as well, and it was not an uncommon practice for one or both of them to slip out at night to the first rancher's headgate (point of diversion from the stream), divert the water to their own crops and return it again at daybreak.

Nocturnal irrigation was popular until the first rancher discovered the trick, and then the war was really on. The rancher of that day defended his water with lead and everything he had behind it. Lives were lost and so much bitterness engendered that the law was forced to take a hand in straightening the matter out.

The antagonists were thereafter hailed into court and their claims considered. The judge apportioned the water as fairly as he could, and decreed the rights by law. From that time on tampering with another rancher's ditches or headgates was adjudged contempt of court and punishable by a large fine and jail sentence.

But the seeds of bitterness and suspicion were already sown. Where water was concerned no man trusted another.

There were still more complaints, which could not be sub-
stantiated, and so another law came into being. Any man
on a ditch could demand that that ditch be policed, and
every man with decreed water, in proportion to the number
of inches he owned, was forced to bear his share of a ditch
rider's salary.

The ditch rider was appointed by the judge. He rode the
ditch each day, measured the water and apportioned it
fairly to the various ranchers. This practice still holds
in the Valley when we have a dry season. During the last
depression it worked an unnecessary financial hardship on
most of the ranchers but I never heard one complain of the
cost. They paid it gladly and cut corners elsewhere.

I was talking over early-day irrigation not so long ago
with a game warden whose mother was one of the first
white children born in Virginia City. He is quite an author-
ity on the subject. I was amused when he chuckled and
said: 'In spite of all the ditch riders and decrees, the man
who lived nearest the head of the creek had the best water
right in those days, and by golly he still has. Men stole
water then and they steal it now. You know that as well
as I do.'

I did know it. Many owners of secondary water rights,
men who are honest in their business dealings, who would
not dream of turning stock onto a neighbor's range to steal
his feed, feel absolutely within their rights if they can
get away with diverting his water for a few hours. They
justify themselves something after the manner of a man
who recently was caught tampering with a neighbor's headgate.

In the course of a heated quarrel the rancher with the first
right out of the creek said: 'This water was decreed before
you and I were born and it was fairly decreed. I'm entitled

to two hundred inches of water and by God, I'm going to have it — or else.'

'It wasn't fairly decreed,' the second rancher exclaimed wrathfully. 'I've seeded forty acres to alfalfa since that decree and now I haven't a drop of water to irrigate it.'

I remember one bitter quarrel which resulted in tragedy soon after I came to Montana. Two homesteaders, a man and a woman, became violent enemies over a disputed water right and dealt each other as much misery as possible. The man had the worst of it. He was a slow-spoken, inarticulate fellow and the woman had a tongue tied in the middle and wagging at both ends. She also had an ungovernable temper and would stand on the ditch bank shrieking invectives each time he got within range of her voice.

When driven too far the man threatened to shut her up if he had to take a gun to do it. One day she disappeared. Her relatives instigated a search and when it was unsuccessful some of them questioned her enemy. He informed them sulkily that he thought she had moved away; he hadn't seen her for days. This explanation seemed a bit thin and the relatives were not satisfied. They called the sheriff in and another search was made, which took in every foot of both homesteads. They found no trace of the woman.

The relatives swore out a warrant for the man's arrest and he was taken to jail. After exhaustive questioning he became confused, broke down and confessed that he had killed his neighbor. He claimed he had put up with all her devilment, but when he caught her attempting to poison the drinking water in his well, he had lost his head and shot her.

He agreed to show the sheriff and his deputy the spot where his victim was buried. When they reached it he pointed out the stump of a tree which he had planted over the grave in so realistic a fashion that none would have suspected its sinister purpose. The sheriff, to his chagrin, recognized the stump as one he had rested against while eating lunch on the day he had searched for the woman's body.

Rainfall and drought have always run in cycles in Montana. On rare occasions there have been periods over a number of years when the rainfall was better than normal, and sufficient in this Valley and in other parts of the state to grow bumper dry-land crops. One of these phenomenal cycles of rainfall was responsible for a tragic land boom that bankrupted thousands of homesteaders and destroyed miles upon miles of virgin range all over the state.

The Homestead Law was one benevolent gesture of the Government's which resulted in tragedy, heartache and disillusionment. On the face of it, it was alluring. Any man with the price of a small filing fee might prove up on a homestead by living upon it for three years, and improving it in that time to the amount of a dollar and twenty-five cents per acre. The improvements could not include a dwelling, but they could include fence, corral, barn, tree culture and a well.

From 1900 on for a number of years the rainfall was a hundred per cent above normal in this part of the state. Dry-land crops were bountiful and the real estate agencies in Eastern States cashed in on the bonanza. They advertised extensively, offering to locate a likely homestead for what seemed a moderate fee. The railroads also advertised, painting glowing pictures of the Land of Promise which appealed to the pioneer-minded in many walks of life. . . . Free land . . . a new life . . . wide horizons.

The picture spread like a prairie fire. Clerks, stenographers, bookkeepers, ministers and discouraged farmers from other states drew out the last penny of their savings and blithely set forth to make a new start on land they had never even seen.

Many of them discovered too late that there was not a drop of water on their newly acquired land, not a shade tree or a splinter of wood for cooking and heating purposes. And even so, almost without exception, they sunk every penny they possessed into improvements, stubbornly determined to make a go of it. They built houses, fences, barns and corrals. They planted trees and tried to dig wells. Wells were their biggest problem. Until they could be dug the homesteaders were forced to haul water in barrels, sometimes as far as twenty miles. And all too few found water once the wells were dug.

The story is told of a city man who met a dry-land farmer hauling his barrels from water. 'How far do you have to haul that water?' the city man asked. 'Ten miles,' the homesteader replied. 'Why don't you dig a well?' the city man wanted to know. 'I've tried,' the homesteader answered grimly. 'Water's just as far that way as this and a lot more expensive.'

The scarcity of water and wood was a terrible blow to the homesteaders, but even this could not dull the edge of their great adventure. They were optimistic souls. They wrested boulders from the earth, plowed up fields and put in crops. It was a survival of the fittest from the start. Some of the white-collar homesteaders, with no knowledge whatever of farming methods, went bankrupt quickly. They were lucky. And wise, as it turned out, for they acknowledged defeat and went back to jobs before the land took its full toll of their courage and will.

Others stayed, harvested a fair crop — enough to break even — for several rainy years, and then came the débâcle. Nature had promoted the land boom and Nature, ever fickle in this country, pulled it down ruthlessly. For three

years drought took over the land. The sun blazed down
with a merciless heat... hot winds blew. Grain lay dor-
mant in the parched, cracked ground. The range burned
up and wells and streams ran dry.

There was another exodus, but still the hardiest of those
homesteaders hung on. They could not forget that cycle
of rainy years and grimly they waited for rain. But the
land was now a monster which held a whiplash over them,
and they paid in back-breaking toil, in sacrifice and in
blasted hopes.

Their money was gone and the land would no longer
yield them a living. They mortgaged their holdings, down
to the last frying-pan and griddle, in order to raise cash
for food and seed. That seed never sprouted. The wind
took the topsoil and piled it like snowdrifts against the
fences. Banks, in self-protection, were forced to foreclose.
In the end six million acres of land were abandoned, either
to banks or to the Government.

The tragedy of it was that nearly all of those homesteaders who had come to Montana with such high hopes left
beaten, discouraged and penniless, sometimes owning little
more than the shirts on their backs. Some of them had
built comfortable homes, spacious barns and good corrals,
but as they left they did not, like Lot's wife, look back with
regret. They deserted the scene of their disaster as they
might have deserted a plague-ridden ship.

Curiously enough, some of them retained their sense of
humor to the end — but it was a grim humor that had its
roots in heartache and despair. I once saw painted in boxcar letters across the side of a deserted homestead this verse:

> *Fifteen miles to water,*
> *Twenty miles to wood;*
> *We're leaving this damn country,*
> *And we're leaving it for good.*

Ten miles distant from this homestead, on the back of a
barn — in boxcar letters too — I read these words:

> *Uncle Sam bet me 320 acres*
> *against a filing fee that I*
> *couldn't stick it out three*
> *years. Uncle Sam won.*

There is one hill in a neighboring county where I have
stood and counted sixteen abandoned homesteads. I never
gaze down on this desolate scene without getting a lump
in my throat. I know the story of many of those bleak,
sagging roofs, broken windows and fences. I know that
high hope lived there and died a stark, tortured death, and
I always wonder what has become of those homesteaders
and their families.

I wonder what became of the young clerk who buried
his wife and their premature son in a coffin fashioned by
his own hands, from boards ripped off the side of his house.
When someone offered a shocked protest he defended his
action passionately. 'Mary hated debt,' he sobbed. 'She
wouldn't let me mortgage this place, even for food. She
wouldn't let me go in debt for a doctor, and a doctor could
have saved her. She wouldn't rest easy in a coffin that
wasn't paid for — *and Mary is going to rest.*'

I wonder what became of the widower farmer who, in
early autumn, walked into a bank, followed by his five
ragged, barefooted children. 'I'm leaving,' he told the
banker. 'You can have my place and welcome. If I was a
single man I'd stick and get the best of that homestead if it
took the rest of my life. But I've got to think of my kids,
and by God, I'm getting them out before another snow flies,
while they still have rags to cover their nakedness.'

I wonder what became of the wife of the bookkeeper who
balanced his last account at the end of a rope hung from

the rafters of his barn. I wonder about the two prim spinster schoolteachers who hopped a freight because they had no money for railroad fare...about the Lutheran minister who tried in vain to trade the equity in his homestead, with all improvements, for a second-hand model-T Ford and who set out on foot when his efforts proved futile.

Nature defrauded all these homesteaders, and they in turn unwittingly defrauded the land. Acre after acre of what had once been good grazing land was plowed up and left to go back to a wilderness of sagebrush and tumbleweed. Buffalo sod and other nutritious native grasses were killed when their roots were destroyed, and they have never come back. The land is still a desolate waste and still worse a menace, for the seeds of sagebrush and tumbleweed, scattered by the wind, have found fertile soil on the range.

The Government has tried to make amends. The Government has fought this gradual encroachment and the stockman has fought it. They have experimented — have planted again and again — in an effort to reclaim abandoned homestead lands, and they are still experimenting, but their efforts as a whole have proved futile. All Man's science and all Man's ingenuity so far have not been able to bring back what Man himself destroyed.

23

The lambs are shipped to market

YESTERDAY we loaded the lambs for market and so wound up our business for the year. The last two weeks have been busy ones for all of us, but especially busy for Tom and the men who took active part in the lamb drive. And now Tom is speeding toward Chicago in the old-fashioned day coach attached to the rear end of a long stock train.

Everyone on the ranch is glad to have this job out of the way, but no one is gladder than Bill, the black bellwether, who leads the lambs to the shipping point. All morning I've heard the jubilant tinkle of his sheep bell, and I've known he was kicking up his heels from sheer relief in the corral across the creek.

It would be impossible to explain the process of shipping without casting Bill in the leading rôle. Not that he appreciates the distinction, for he is an abused and reluctant actor in the big event of the season. His lot is not so hard as he'd like to have us believe, for he works only two weeks in the year, and the rest of the time he leads the life of Riley. He ambles about the tree-shaded corral with the yearling calves and gorges himself on hay. He slakes his thirst in the crystal waters of Wigwam Creek and sleeps in peace on its mossy banks. For fifty weeks he's a Big Shot, bullying the calves or cavorting with them, as suits his lordly pleasure.

Two weeks of work at shipping time is a small price to pay for all this luck, but Bill doesn't think so. Bill has a grievance: he hates lambs. He tells us about it each year when a stock truck backs through the gates of his corral and prepares to haul him to the Forest. He knows where he's going and how disagreeable his task will be. His liquid brown eyes reproach us and bleats that are meant to soften our hearts come tremulously from his throat.

When the camp-tender slips a halter around his neck he stiffens his legs and rears back rebelliously. His bleats gain volume and eloquence as he calls on his friends the calves to witness this shameful betrayal. But the crowning ignominy takes place when he's unceremoniously boosted into the truck and tied to the sideboards. He gives up then and assumes an air of injured dignity, which he maintains until he has led his troublesome charges all the way from our headquarters camp on the Forest to the stockyards at the shipping point.

Innocently enough, it was I who launched Bill on his

career of range bellwether. He only held down that job a
year, and he has himself to thank for the circumstances
which forced him into the humbler one he now finds so distasteful.

Bill started life as a 'bum' (orphan or twin raised on a
bottle at the home ranch). He was dropped in the last days
of lambing and his mother died while giving him birth. So
late in the season there was no other ewe to adopt him. We
already had ten 'bums' at the ranch — all we could spare
milk for — and I'm sure he would have been put out of
the way had he not been a black lamb.

The black sheep is a valuable ally in the sheep industry
and no woolgrower ever has as many as he needs. This type
of sheep is a mystery, whose very existence nobody seems
able to explain. We have never owned a black ram but we
get close to twenty black lambs each year, mostly from
white-face ewes.

Custom has fixed their mission in life, which is a matter of
arithmetic. In every herd there is supposed to be one black
sheep or marker for each one hundred white. Sheep seldom
stray alone. When a marker is missing, nine times out of
ten a hundred or more ewes will be missing as well. It would
be impossible for the herder to count out his flock on the
range, but it is no trick for him to stand on a hillside and
keep track of the markers. So long as they are all accounted
for, he can be reasonably sure that his herd is intact.

The demand for black sheep has always exceeded the
supply, but I was not concerned with this fact when Tom
walked through the gate with Bill tucked under his arm.
I was dismayed and eyed him with stony disapproval. The
chore boy is supposed to look after the bums, but somehow
or other it falls to my lot in the end.

The chore boy is busy getting his garden in at this season.

The garden is a quarter-mile up the canyon from the house and it is a very large garden. It has to be large because it supplies the ranch not only with summer vegetables but with winter vegetables — beets, carrots, rutabegas, potatoes, parsnips and onions — as well.

The bums are supposed to be fed five times a day in the first month of their life. The chore boy gets tied up with his planting and forgets the feeding schedules. But the lambs don't forget. They know their schedules to the minute. You could set a watch by them. When it's time to eat they rush the back gate in a body, and make life unbearable for everyone in the house. Their blats are earsplitting, and they rattle and bang and butt on the gate until it's impossible to ignore them.

I try. I tell myself that it isn't my job, that the chore boy will be along pretty soon. But I put up with the racket just so long, and end by warming the bottles and fighting it out through the mesh of the woven-wire fence. It's a messy disagreeable job. They're so eager to get at the milk quickly that they jerk and twist on the nipples, and I've never yet fed a bunch of bums without being either splattered or deluged with milk.

One more bum was just one more annoyance. Small wonder that I wasn't pleased to see Bill. But he won me over, and soon at that. He was such a lovable lamb — so cocky and independent. I liked the way he had of getting down to business with his bottle. No foolishness there. Bill never twisted or pulled. He simply spread his small knobby legs, wrapped his muzzle around the nipple, sucked lustily for a few moments and then backed away with whiskers of milk jutting ludicrously from either side of his mouth.

Curiously enough, the very trait which won me over was the cause of Bill's undoing. Good manners were not responsible for his restraint, but plain, unvarnished greed; the avid determination to get the last drop for himself. He used his head, did Bill. No spilled milk for him.

As time went by I became deeply attached to Bill, and keenly interested in his future. There were two careers open to him. He could be thrown into the herd as a marker or, if someone had the patience to train him, he could become a bellwether. Markers are commonplace, but there's a decided distinction to being a bellwether. There will be fifteen markers in each herd of that many hundred sheep, and only one lead-sheep. It soon became plain that Bill was destined to lead, and I offered to train him.

An outstanding characteristic of sheep is their overweening desire for a leader. There are always sheep bolder than the rest. Sometimes the leader will be a wise old ewe, selected from the rank and file, but more often the choice will be a 'bum.' The courage of the bums is explained perhaps by the fact that they are seldom exposed to danger until such time as confidence has been instilled into them.

Once the sheep pick a leader there is no place they would not follow him. Of course their confidence is often misplaced and they must suffer the consequence.

Bill took to his job as a duck takes to water. There was a swagger and charm to his leadership. When his training had been completed he was thrown into a herd of ewes, and he had not been with them a week before they would follow him blindly — across narrow pole bridges, which normally sheep loathe, across rushing streams and, as we were to discover, even through fire. On this occasion Bill's greed betrayed his herd and caused a pile-up.

When I heard the details of this pile-up, I felt largely responsible. I'd trained him to lead with pellets of cottonseed cake, and there I made a mistake. His love for this tidbit went beyond bounds, and he'd cooperate so long as it was used for a bait. Nothing else held his interest long. He might follow a crust of bread or a graham cracker half-heartedly over some smooth, pleasant trail, but only cotton-seed cake could entice him across a bridge or through running water.

Obviously he had to learn to take the more difficult trails, and just as obviously I baited him with cake. Bill had me over a barrel. I'd promised to train him and couldn't back down. But soon it took two pellets to get him across a bridge — then three — then four. I was forced to increase the ration and hold it plainly in sight or he wouldn't budge. I trained him — no lead-sheep was ever trained better — but in the process I learned what a glutton he was.

He got no cake when he was turned out on the range, and how he must have missed it! Cottonseed cake is expensive feed, reserved for the drop bands because of its milk-producing qualities. During lambing it is stored in small makeshift sheds all over the range. Shortly after Bill was put to work, one of these sheds was struck by lightning and it burned to the ground. There was still around half a ton of cake inside when the building collapsed.

On that day the herder of Bill's band was grazing his sheep just over the hill. He saw the dense spiral of smoke, became alarmed and pushed his sheep to the crest of the hill to investigate. Just then the cottonseed cake began to burn.

Bill had been ambling along in the fore of the sheep and suddenly he stopped short, sniffed the pungent smell of the smoldering cake and made a frantic dive in the direction of the shed. His craving was short-lived. Before he had barged very far into the red-hot débris he leaped into the air, veered and made his escape. But not before half the herd had followed in his wake and piled up.

Fifty sheep perished, and but for the quick work of the herder many more would have been lost. A number were badly burned and limped about for weeks. They hadn't learned a thing from their experience. They continued to follow Bill with the same blind faith. But Bill had learned. From that day on nothing could induce him to work against a wind that was laden with wood smoke.

This shortcoming, when reported by the herder, caused us alarm. If Bill struck a smoke-laden wind he might turn tail and lead his band into all sorts of trouble. Tom took no chances. He had Bill hauled back to the ranch and announced that he intended to ship him with the rest of the lambs that fall. I protested indignantly. Bill — into mutton chops? I became so distressed that Tom relented and invented a new job for him. In the past any bellwether handy had led the lambs to the stockyards at the shipping point. Now Bill was to have the job.

Bill must have believed himself in luck when he was first brought home. He had never relished the idea of foraging for food anyhow. He didn't know what was in store for him that first fall he was loaded into a truck and hauled up to the Forest, and he was no more than mildly concerned. But he knows now!

Bill took his last trip to the Forest two weeks ago. He's eight years old and deserves to be retired. I'm not keen about watching the lambs cut away from their mothers, but it was curtains for Bill and I wanted to watch his last performance. I drove to the Forest with Tom.

The morning was perfect. Autumn had laid the touch of Midas on the lower Forest with every conceivable shading of gold. Cottonwoods and quaking aspens and willows

stood out in saffron splendor against the dull bronze of rolling grassy slopes, while the paler gold of wild currant and
sarvice berries framed the flaming orange of native brush.
A breath-taking spectacle of gorgeousness which can thrill
me still, but no longer fool me. I know it for what it is —
an interval of color . . . a miracle that has come too soon and
will not linger long.

Autumn, cloaked in such lovely garb, can't make me forget that there's a hint of snow in the air; that low fleecy
clouds ride before the wind, like flecks of foam on a sullen
sea; that I have only to raise my eyes to the distant peaks
and I shall find them already patterned in white.

It was warm when we left the home ranch that morning
but bitterly cold before we climbed the four thousand feet
to our Forest allotment. The men were standing about the
corrals waiting for the Boss with the collars of their sheepskin coats turned high about their necks. Their breath
steamed out in little spirals and their faces were ruddy with
cold.

Cutting the lambs is quite a ceremony. All our sheep are
herded near the corrals at headquarters camp, so close together that it keeps their herders jumping to prevent a
mixup. A mixup would be a calamity, since it would mean
corralling and separating all sheep mixed according to their
various brands. The bands, therefore, are brought into the
corrals one by one and herded back to their grazing areas as
fast as the cutting and culling is accomplished.

The ewes were fractious that morning, determined not to
leave their lambs behind. The mountains resounded with
frantic, protesting blats. It was almost impossible to drive
them away from the corrals. The herders and wranglers
shouted and swore, the dogs raced and barked, but the distracted mothers kept breaking away from the outgoing

herds and returning to the fence which shut them away from
their lambs.

I saw one old ewe dash back and miraculously find her
lamb through the panel. She nosed the little fellow, and as
I watched I could have sworn that a pucker of anxiety between her eyes smoothed out, in the moment before the dogs
caught up and chased her away, into an expression of
beatific relief.

As usual this little scene got the best of me. I told myself
sternly that what I took for mother love was nothing more
than instinct; that my sympathy was wasted because the
ewe would forget that she'd ever had a lamb in a day or two.
I brought forth all my timeworn arguments, tried to think
in terms of lamb chops ... and couldn't. The poignancy of
that reunion had spoiled the day for me ...

I quit the corrals and went up to the headquarters camp
to help the camp-tender prepare dinner for the crew.

The cabin at the headquarters camp is a primitive struc-
ture: a one-room log house with a dirt floor and roof. There
is a crude bunk in one corner and a sheet-iron camp stove in
another. Two benches and a table stand in the middle of
the room and the walls are lined with cupboards. These cupboards hold the canned goods, dried fruit, flour, sugar,
tobacco and 'snoose' with which the camp-tender supplies
the herders in summer.

The camp-tender's temper was ruffled that morning.
He felt abused and put upon. Tom had promised to bring
up a man to cook and drive the chuck truck for the lamb
drive but had been unable to find one. The camp-tender was
gloomily peeling potatoes, dropping the grimy, half-washed
tubers into a kettle which he held between his knees.

He cast a hopeful eye in my direction. I knew what he
was thinking and I wanted to laugh ... *The missus is a bum*

*cook, but who cares on a lamb drive? ... She can handle a truck
as well as me ...* I saw the gloom settle back on his face as
he discarded this happy avenue of escape. Turning it over
in his mind he remembered reluctantly that the Missus
couldn't wrangle camp stove or bed-rolls ... and she
couldn't unload and set up tents.

'Looks like I'm always the one to get hooked for this job,'
he grumbled.

'That's what you get for bragging about your cooking,' I
teased, eyeing the potatoes doubtfully. But he looked so
abused and forlorn that I impulsively offered to prepare
dinner. He took me up like a flash, grabbed his cap and set
out for the corrals on a lope, as though he feared I might
change my mind.

The cutting of the lambs went on all through that day.
One by one the herds were driven back to their grazing areas
and just before dusk the job was done.

Several thousand half-weaned lambs were huddled
wretchedly together to await the start in the morning.
That many lambs can make a lot of noise. Tom had pitched
our tepee as far from the corral as he could find level ground,
but it was not far enough. All night long and far into the
morning those tremulous blats penetrated our canvas shelter
and kept me awake. I stared into the vibrating darkness
and swore (as I've sworn before) that this would be my last
night on the Forest — at shipping time anyway.

It seemed to me that I had just dozed off when the camp
came noisily to life. With the first blur of dawn men began
tearing down tents and tepees and hoisting them on the
chuck truck. As I dressed, dragging my icy clothes onto my
shivering body, I heard the rattle of a camp stove ... the
clatter of skillets and pans ... the dull thud of bed-rolls ...
and the final adjusting of the truck's end gate. I knew the
loading was done.

The cabin was deserted when I got there. The men had left for the corrals and the camp-tender had started the chuck truck down the mountain trail. The truck always keeps in advance of the drive, stopping at some agreed point to prepare the noon meal, and going from there to the camp planned for that night.

It was warm in the cabin and I was loathe to leave it, but I had promised to bring Bill down to the corrals, so I hastily gulped a cup of coffee and set out to get him. Bill was tied to the wheel of a buckboard and his posture was one of dejection. He greeted me with a feeble, wavering blat and turned his head away.

He was more obstinate than usual that day, I suppose because I had been chosen to lead him. He refused to budge. I jerked and pulled, but I had not the strength to move him. In the end I had to go to the corral and ask a herder to help me.

The herder took his halter and dragged him within ten feet of the lamb corral. Bill flashed me one last despairing glance and then his body went rigid. His ears laid back and his eyes rolled wildly. He had heard the first creak of the gate which would release his tormentors. The gate swung open and several lambs leaped forth. They stood hesitantly for a moment and then they spied Bill.

Bewildered and hungry, the lambs rushed him. On and on they came, worse than a swarm of bees. They sucked his head, his legs, his ears. They butted and jerked — they came in such numbers that they knocked poor Bill to his knees. And so they would persecute him until the shipping point was reached. No wonder he hated them; no wonder he would be glad to be rid of them.

Tom and I watched the lamb drive start down the mountain and then we went back to load our bed and tepee into the car. I was stiff with cold by now and not sorry to be heading for the ranch. But we were not yet on our way. We caught up with the drive and Tom stopped to speak with one of the herders. He was on the point of climbing back into the car when another herder shouted for a halt and gestured wildly toward a grove of quaking aspen trees. A ewe had come back and got what she came for. We saw her skip nimbly into the grove with a lamb at her heels. The dogs brought her back and turned her lamb again into the drive. And we had the mother for a back-seat passenger until we reached the ranch.

She looked so disconsolate and beaten, lying there on the floor of the car. I could not help wishing that she had been as smart as another ewe which, not so many years before, had stolen her lamb and got away with it.

This ewe broke out of her herd and followed the drive for a distance of forty miles. She was canny enough to keep out of sight until the third night, when she slipped into the band, recovered her lamb and returned in triumph to the Forest. The curious part was that while she recovered her lamb by stealth, she returned quite openly, seeming to know that no herder is going to travel forty-odd miles, even if he could leave his flock to do so, to return a lone lamb to the fold.

I did not see much more of the lamb drive until it reached the shipping point. I was busy in the intervening days. I had two separate outfits to pack for Tom — work clothes for the trip, and 'store clothes' to be worn in Chicago. Two other woolgrowers were shipping with us. Their wives and I had to prepare and pack lunches to last for six days. The shippers could cook their breakfasts on the round-bellied heating stove in the rear of the coach, but the rest of the meals were packed at home. It took a lot of planning.

The lunches of the first two days could include pies, cakes, salad, fried chicken and baked meats, but working out the lunches for the remainder of the trip was quite a problem. These had to consist of food that would not spoil readily. And each lunch had to be bountiful since the party included three herders who were taken along to help care for the sheep when they were unloaded at the feed stations on the way.

The last lap of the lamb drive goes over fifteen miles of busy highway and is by far the worst. Passing cars frighten the lambs and they're hard to handle. A much larger crew is needed for this stretch, and Tom leaves home the morning of the day before loading to help. I take his lunch and bags down to the shipping point early next day. Consequently I'm always on hand for the loading. I'd skip it if I could.

I hate to see those poor foolish lambs leap trustingly up the chute in the wake of the bellwether. However necessary this method of loading may be, it is still a cheap trick, a betrayal of faith. Tom laughs when I say this and I try to laugh at myself. I know lambs were raised to be slaughtered — that people must be fed. I know too that it is better for the lambs to follow the bellwether quietly into the chute than to be prodded and pushed and dogged. But it's no use. I've never been able to build up an immunity to shipping and I never shall ... I can't argue myself into believing that Tom's method is right or fair.

Yesterday I stood on the lowest rung of the loading corral and watched Bill load his first deck. He ran swiftly up the slanted chute to the lower deck of the stock car and hesitated for a moment at the door. The lambs pressed him closely, craning their heads to see what it was all about. Bill allowed their curiosity to reach white heat and then he ambled slowly into the car and moved with large unconcern to the far end. The lambs moved too. When the car was full Bill sneaked along the side and made his escape from the door. He seemed cocky and pleased as he leaped forth to freedom with the air of a man who thoroughly liked his job.

There were thirty-five double-deck cars in the two-section train that pulled out of the little mountain stock yards several hours later. Tom, the two other woolgrowers, and three herders stood on the platform at the rear of the train, waving good-bye to a cheering crowd.

Tin dogs (cans strung on baling wire) rattled frantically, and hats were thrown into the air. As the long train gained momentum the din increased. Good-natured warnings of outmoded vintage mingled lustily with shouts of good luck and good-bye — *Don't take any brass nickels! — Don't let those Chicago slickers sell you a gold brick!* And then one herder cupped his hands about his mouth and gave voice to the hope that was uppermost in everyone's heart, *'Fifteen-cent lambs!'* he shrieked. *'Whee-ee-ee! Fifteen-cent lambs!'*

And now our year is done. Gazing out across the burnished slopes of hills that spell home to me, I know that it has been a good year. Yesterday a herder cupped his hands about his mouth and shouted, *'Fifteen-cent lambs!'* This morning I wonder ... It's too much to hope for, and yet — just last week a shipment of Wyoming range lambs brought thirteen cents a pound on the Chicago market. A normal profit would mean so much to the woolgrower. It would mean that a great industry could be stabilized again; that the sheepman could build up his flocks for the first time in years; that he could raise more wool and better wool ...

Outside my windows a sudden gust of wind sweeps through the cottonwoods, bringing a shower of gold to the

ground. In another week those trees will be stark and bare
... snow will come and blanket the ranch ... fierce winds
will hurl that snow into drifts. Then winter will take over
the land. It will be cold — bitterly cold. ...

I think of our herds spread out on the other side of the
hills, and strangely I do not picture the fleece on the backs
of our sheep as wool. I see more and more spindles turning;
more and more yards of cloth and yarn fall smoothly off the
loom to be transformed into suits and dresses, into socks
and blankets and underwear that will help keep my coun-
trymen warm.

THE END